OVERCOMING
OBSTACLES

A FIGHT TO THE FINISH

TIFFANY C. EDGECOMBE

LARGO, MARYLAND
USA

Christian Living Books, Inc.
P. O. Box 7584
Largo, MD 20792
christianlivingbooks.com

ISBN Paperback 9781562292423

ISBN Small Group Study Guide 9781562292461

ISBN eBook 9781562292430

Printed in the United States of America.

CONTENTS

FOREWORD

Overcoming Obstacles: A Fight to the Finish is a must read for every Believer, not only for those who have become disillusioned due to the dark cloud of discouragement and challenged by the obstacles of life. There is a profound sense of encouragement that the author infuses through this book that propels the reader to not only run the best possible race he or she can run but to finish what God has begun within.

Life is a journey – a race to the end. Those who are diligent will reap the rewards of implementing the disciplines outlined throughout this book. This is a prescription to stir your faith, starve your doubt and fears and impose the Kingdom of God wherever you are.

Of course you won't get far if you don't suit up for the journey ahead as the author skillfully weaves every Christian discipline into the fabric of this book. Faith, prayer, love and patience are just a few of the highlights magnified page after page. However, the recurring theme of faith propelled me to face my giants and overcome my obstacles.

From my first encounter with this work, I envisioned my congregation reading this book together. What a powerful tool that helps Believers to solidify their faith in God and seek out deliverances from a biblical perspective.

There's one thing for sure, God's voice will become clearer and more discernable as you turn the pages of this book. It's time for you to break out of your cocoons and embrace the sense of empowerment to walk at a higher level of sacrifice and obedience.

Tiffany Edgecombe, the author, compels us to be sacrificial in our service of each other, as we push pass our comfort to stay steadfast.

Pastor Mario Moxey
Senior Pastor
Bahamas Harvest Church
Nassau, Bahamas

ACKNOWLEDGMENTS

There are so many that have poured into my life and greatly contributed to the successful completion of this book.

First, to my loving Heavenly Father, Who created me and sent me here to planet Earth to accomplish His purpose for my life. I thank You for the obstacles You have brought me to and through throughout the years. Each and every one taught me a valuable, eternal lesson that I now have the opportunity to share with the world. Your love and protection has been evident in every season of my life. Thank You for Your still, small voice that constantly guides me every day, reminding me that You promised "never to leave me, nor forsake me." I love you now and forever, my Ever Present Help!

Next, to my caring and affectionate husband, Adrian: I am truly blessed being married to you. Every day, I look at you and I want to be a better person because of the way you live your life. You have faced so many obstacles and overcame them with God's help. You never ask "why me" but use each challenge as an opportunity to glorify God. You encourage me daily, to never give up and to speak life over each situation. Your life is a powerful testimony that encourages me, and others I'm sure, to keep pressing and running our race with purpose and excellence, because you are a man of purpose and excellence. Thank you for loving and supporting me in the writing and editing of this book and in everything I attempt to do. I am stronger because of you and I love you more than words can say!

To my two princes, Arron and Israel: You both have brought me so much joy and excitement. Every day I wake up I want to do what I have been called to do and be a better Christian because I want to leave a legacy for you to follow. You are growing up to be such fine, young Christian men and I am so proud of your many accomplishments. When I am faced with an obstacle, I want to overcome it so that you can see that "with God, all things are possible!" I thank God for the life lessons He has taught me through your lives. Love you, Wugsy and Raeli!

To my parents, Rosemary Braynen and Anthony Braynen: You have been my biggest cheerleaders throughout my entire life. You always encouraged me to reach for the sky and celebrated my every success and picked me up when I have stumbled along the way. I feel your love every day and it motivates me to be the best I can be. Thank you so much for being loyal and supportive. I love you both!

To my brother, Trystian: Thank you for the support that you show in your own special way. I'm grateful to know that you always "have my back". Love you, 'lil bro!

To my pastors, Pastors Mario and Erika Moxey: Your years of sacrificial service and undying commitment to the cause of Christ have motivated me to be all I can be and do all I can do for God. Your life's message has caused me to be a woman of faith, because faith is contagious. I can never stay in my comfort zone, because you constantly challenge me to go beyond the box and seize the moments in my life. Thank you for all that you do!

To my life coach, Minister Kim Sweeting: You are truly a blessing to me, and the Body of Christ at large. From the moment we connected, the light of God in your life began to shine through the dark clouds of fear and discouragement that were trying to overshadow me at the time. Your words were so timely, and our weekly sessions really helped me to regain my focus on the task at hand. You held me accountable to the completion of this book, which has now become a reality! I thank God for you, and thank you!

INTRODUCTION

The Race We Face

*W*e all have been called to run this race we call life. Long before we were born, God chose or predestined us to run a specific course for Him to manifest His glory on the earth.

> Therefore, since we are surrounded by such a great cloud of witnesses, let us throw off everything that hinders and the sin that so easily entangles. And let us run with perseverance the race marked out for us, fixing our eyes on Jesus, the pioneer and perfecter of faith.
>
> (Hebrews 12:1-2 NIV)

The scripture above tells us that there were other runners before us who have already ran and finished their course and they are now making up that cloud of witnesses cheering us on from their Heavenly reward as we run our race and fulfill our mission for God on the earth. These people include Abraham, Isaac, Jacob, Moses, Rahab, Joshua, David, Gideon and all of the other men and women of the Bible who came to earth and accomplished what they were sent here to do.

Now it's our time to run our race. However, there is a choice we must make: will we run with God as our Coach and Instructor or will we attempt to run this race of life in our own strength and with our self-made road map? Sadly, many people are completely unaware that God has a plan for their lives. These people are running but they don't know where they are going.

Life, without God, is like running through a maze. Remember, the paper maze games we played as children? We tried one route and if we reached a dead end, we tried another path to the exit. It is the same experience people will have when they begin running without the God-ordained road map for their lives. They run around and around and usually end up in a place that is impossible to pass. So they try another route and may appear to be making some progress only to discover that they are headed toward another dead-end. They may have some successes along their pathway, but they never experience true fulfillment and passion, because these come from knowing God.

On the outside, some may really seem to have it all: success, fame, and fortune; but on the inside they are frustrated, unhappy, depressed and directionless – they are empty! How many famous people have we seen who appeared to have everything anyone could possibly want, but fall victim to drugs, alcohol, depression and premature death?

This is because the race of life was designed by God Himself – the Master Creator of the universe! Any attempt to run without Him as our Navigator is an exercise in futility and will end in fruitlessness.

Life's race for those who have connected with their Navigator, through a relationship with His Son, Jesus Christ, is "not a walk in the park" either. No matter who we are, we will experience ups and downs and many obstacles in this race we face. But the difference is Christians are aware that they have a specific destination. With God as their Navigator, they can be successfully piloted through life's frustrations, disappointments and setbacks. An obstacle is an impediment, roadblock or setback that we encounter in our course that is intended to delay or completely prevent us from arriving at God's destination for our lives. Therefore, our race may be likened to an obstacle course. There is an expected end, but we must go through some challenges, learning how to overcome to press on through our process. When we conquer one challenge, there may be a flat road to catch our breath, for a moment, until we arrive at the next obstacle that we must learn to overcome by God's power. Some obstacles may require climbing, others may require crawling, and yet with others we may find ourselves holding on for dear life.

However, even though we all will face obstacles as we run our respective races, for the Christian, God's overcoming power is available to us to rise above each and every one of them. God's grace, which is His supernatural enabling power, provides us with what we need to be victorious in the race of our lives. We have His Holy Spirit dwelling within us to lead and guide us on the path that He has laid out for us. The most important thing is He knows our destination and shows us the best way to get there. There may be some lions and snakes along the way, but He has given us the power and authority to trample every one of them under our feet, according to Psalm 91:13. As Christians, we are guaranteed victory because of Christ's finished work on the cross. Therefore, we can run with purpose, assured that God knows where we are headed and will let us know what we are to do during our journey and when we get there!

As you read this book, keep in mind that your race is an individual one. You are competing against yourself because you and only you can run the race that God has set before you. Therefore, if you want to be successful, you must stay in your lane and focus on your own race. Don't get distracted by others who may seem to be ahead of you or appear to be accomplishing more during any stage of the race. It may be that their finish line is ahead of ours. Our job is to follow the instructions of our Commanding Officer to finish successfully before we are called to our eternal reward.

Additionally, none of us know exactly how long our race will be. Many of us have been running for a while, but have we been productive along the way? Some of us may be called to run a short distance. Others may be called to run a middle distance race. Still others may be called to endure longer distances such as a marathon. The length and duration of the course we have been assigned is not as important as the impact we make on this world as we run our race and represent the Kingdom of God with distinction! Be assured that God has empowered us to accomplish our purpose in life no matter how long or short our distance may be.

The starter's gun has already been fired. Are you still in the starting blocks? Your race has already begun. On your mark, get set, GO!

CHAPTER

OVERCOMING OBSTACLES

This life we live is filled with hills and valleys. It is not a straight road, but one that is filled with obstacles.

> Be sober, be vigilant; because your adversary the devil, as a roaring lion, walketh about, seeking whom he may devour. (1 Peter 5:8)

> Finally, my brethren, be strong in the Lord and in the power of His might. Put on the whole armor of God, that you may be able to stand against the wiles of the devil. For we do not wrestle against flesh and blood, but against principalities, against powers, against the rulers of the darkness of this age, against spiritual hosts of wickedness in the heavenly places. (Ephesians 6:10-12 NKJV)

These verses confirm that we are in a war and every day we have to fight in order to finish our course. There are spiritual forces around us that are warring against us daily to get us to become discouraged, to throw in the towel and stop running our race for our Great King. Sometimes the attack may come in the form of a sickness, a troubled relationship, a financial challenge or any situation that brings with it discomfort, fear, worry, doubt or pain. It seems that the closer we get to God in our walk with Him, the more trials and obstacles we face.

> Yet in all these things we are more than conquerors through Him who loved us. (Romans 8:37)

Sometimes when we face overwhelming odds, we struggle to embrace this "more than conquering designation" and we wonder if we can live the victorious life that Jesus died to give us.

How do we overcome the obstacles we face?

The apostle Paul was a great example of someone who faced many obstacles as he advanced the gospel of Christ. Initially, he was a persecutor of the Church. However, after his Damascus road conversion experience and the subsequent beginning of his preaching ministry, there was an all-out attempt to force him to abort his mission.

I believe Paul's life was full of obstacles because of the heavy mantle God had placed on his life – the mantle of carrying the gospel of God's grace to the gentiles. It was because of Paul's dedicated work and service to God that we today are also partakers of the grace of God. The devil didn't want this gospel to reach as far as us today, so Paul was beaten and flogged, ambushed, rioted against, misunderstood, falsely accused, imprisoned and shipwrecked all in an attempt to prevent him from finishing his course. As a result, Paul had to fight his way through to the finish line of the race that was set before him.

But how was he able to do this? I think the key is discovered in his letter from his jail cell to the Philippian church. In the midst of all his struggles, his being misjudged and misunderstood, Paul pens the following words:

> Celebrate God all day, every day. I mean, revel in him! Make it as clear as you can to all you meet that you're on their side, working with them and not against them. Help them see that the Master is about to arrive. He could show up any minute! Don't fret or worry. Instead of worrying, pray. Let petitions and praises shape your worries into prayers, letting God know your concerns. Before you know it, a sense of God's wholeness, everything coming together for good, will come and settle you down. It's wonderful what happens when Christ displaces worry at the center of your life. Summing it all up, friends, I'd say you'll do best by filling your minds and meditating on things true,

noble, reputable, authentic, compelling, gracious—the best, not the worst; the beautiful, not the ugly; things to praise, not things to curse. Put into practice what you learned from me, what you heard and saw and realized. Do that, and God, who makes everything work together, will work you into his most excellent harmonies.

(Philippians 4:4-9 MSG)

Four lessons from Paul's life

1. Celebrate!
Paul tells us that in the midst of difficulties, it's time for a celebration! He says when things seem their worst, it's time to sing, it's time to dance, it's time to throw a party, because we know this:

> He who calls you is able to keep you from falling and present us faultless in the presence of His glory with exceeding joy. (Jude 1:24)

So instead of complaining, celebrate! It's a conscious choice that we have to make. We can choose to look at the circumstances and give the obvious response of complaining, nitpicking, worrying, and being afraid, or we can choose to look unto Jesus Who is "the author and finisher of our faith," and celebrate because we are fully convinced that all will be well, and by faith all is well. We recognize that Jesus started this work in us and He is the One Who will bring it to completion. Paul recognized this truth. He knew Jesus had him covered, so he chose to stand on the promises of God and celebrate!

2. Pray and praise instead of worry!
Paul gives us the cure for worry, which is praying – letting God know our concerns – and praising – thanking Him in advance for how He is going to take care of our concerns. Paul was in jail and didn't know how things would turn out, but he knew Who was watching over him. So, he prayed about it and praised God in spite of what he saw and left it in the hands of the God Who could do anything but fail. Again, there is a choice to make: will we worry or will we pray and praise? If we worry, then worry is at the center of our lives. If we pray and praise

God during trials, it shows that Christ is in His rightful place at the center of our lives. Who is at the center of your life today? Is it worry or is it Christ? The answer to that question will determine if you will overcome what you're facing and move to the next level or go round and round the mulberry bush and remain stagnant in the race.

3. Meditate on the good and not the bad!

Paul tells us that we have to reprogram our minds. Too often, we place the focus of our thought life on the negative things we see, instead of the good that God intends to bring out of the bad. It is time to look beyond the circumstances and see God's purpose and what He intends to accomplish through the pain.

> I want to report to you, friends, that my imprisonment here has had the opposite of its intended effect. Instead of being squelched, the Message has actually prospered. All the soldiers here and everyone else too, found out that I'm in jail because of this Messiah. That piqued their curiosity, and now they've learned all about Him. Not only that, but most of the followers of Jesus here have become far more sure of themselves in the faith than ever, speaking out fearlessly about God, about the Messiah. (Philippians 1:12-14 MSG)

There was purpose in Paul's pain, and instead of focusing on the prison, he focused on the purpose being fulfilled as a result.

Do we see the purpose that God wants to fulfill in our lives as a result of the obstacles we face? Do we meditate on the things to praise God for and not the things to curse? Paul encouraged us to follow his example in Philippians. He said, "put it into practice, and watch God work us into His most excellent harmonies" – work it out for GOOD!

I believe that as Paul was encouraging the Philippian church, he was encouraging himself. He was preaching to himself as much as he was preaching to them, so that he could keep on running his race and fight to the finish.

> And I'm going to keep that celebration going because I know how it's going to turn out. Through your faithful prayers and the generous response of the Spirit of Jesus Christ, everything He wants to do in and through me will be done. I can hardly wait to continue on my course. I

> don't expect to be embarrassed in the least. On the contrary, everything happening to me in this jail only serves to make Christ more accurately known, regardless of whether I live or die. They didn't shut me up; they gave me a pulpit. (Philippians 1:18-20 MSG)

What a remarkable statement of faith and trust in God, and a revelation that could have only come from the throne room of God as Paul sat in that jail cell. This happened all because he chose to meditate on the good and not the bad! He saw through his spiritual eyes how it was going to work out. He knew that he had a work to fulfill and that this imprisonment was just a roadblock that he had to get pass so that he could continue to run his race. Suppose Paul chose to only see the negative and gave up? We may not have had two-thirds of the New Testament.

4. Be content… no matter what!
Paul further encourages the Philippian church, and by extension us, to be content and at peace in whatever situations we find ourselves in.

> Actually, I don't have a sense of needing anything personally. I've have learned by now to be quite content whatever my circumstances. I'm just as happy with little as with much, with much as with little. I've found the recipe for being happy whether full or hungry, hands full or hands empty. Whatever I have, wherever I am, I can make it through anything in the One who makes me who I am.
>
> (Philippians 4:11-13 MSG)

In other words, "I can do all things, through Christ who strengthens me." There will be times when we have plenty and times when we don't have as much, but this does not change our position in Christ. Therefore, we should not become uneasy when our circumstances change and shift the focus off of our race, because we can accomplish all things through Christ. It has nothing to do with what we have or where we are, but everything to do with who we are in Him! He is more than enough!

Other Biblical writers have also weighed in on how to overcome the obstacles we face.

5

Remember... God has you covered

The prophet Isaiah reveals a powerful truth that gives us hope as we run this race and fight to the finish. God promises us:

> No weapon that can hurt us has ever been forged. Any accuser who takes you to court will be dismissed as a liar. This is what God's servants can expect. I'll see to it that everything works out for the best. God's decree. (Isaiah 54:17 MSG)

What a blessed assurance from God. When we face obstacles, we can fight to the finish, because we know God is fighting for us. He assures us that there isn't a weapon that has been formed that can hurt us. He promises that He will personally see to it that everything works out for the best. We have His personal guarantee! It does not matter how dark it gets or how bad it looks, God has got us and the best is still yet to come.

Count it all joy!

The apostle James also had his contribution to make concerning how we overcome obstacles.

> Consider it a sheer gift, friends, when tests and challenges come at you from all sides. You know that under pressure, your faith-life is forced into the open and shows its true colors. So don't try to get out of anything prematurely. Let it do its work so you become mature and well-developed, not deficient in any way. (James 1:2-4 MSG)

When we face obstacles, the real us comes to the surface. We begin to see if we are living by faith or not. When pressed, what's on the inside comes out. If we have been meditating on God and His Word, we see faith and victory. If we have been meditating on anything else, fear, worry, doubt, and hopelessness come out. The nature of our relationship with God is exposed during trials.

So let us make a commitment that we will still have joy in the midst of pain, because joy comes from the presence of God. Let's press through and finish the fight so that we can be well developed and not deficient in any way.

God has the final say!

As we face trials, we have to recognize that it is not about us, personally, but it is because of God's purpose on the inside of us that we have been destined to fulfill. This purpose is so important that the enemy of our souls will try to derail us at every turn. That is why Peter tells us…

> Be sober and vigilant, because our adversary, the devil, walketh around like a roaring lion seeking whom he may devour. (1 Peter 5:8 NKJV)

He can't devour everyone. If you are under the Blood of Jesus, he can't devour you; but you must always be on guard. Things may get bad sometimes, but you can keep on running, because you know that ultimate victory is yours through Jesus Christ. Peter further states…

> Keep your guard up. You're not the only one plunged into these hard times. It's the same with Christians all over the world. So keep a firm grip on the faith. The suffering won't last forever. It won't be long before this generous God who has great plans for us in Christ – eternal and glorious plans they are! – will have you put together and on your feet for good. He gets the last word, yes, he does.
>
> (1 Peter 5:9-11 MSG)

That's why we can fight to the finish, because we know God has the final say. Let's not focus on what's happening to us, but rather on what's happening in us during our trials – the growth, the character being shaped, and the strengthening of our spiritual muscles. Overcoming obstacles does not come without a fight, a mental determination to press coupled with God's supernatural enabling power (His grace) to defeat the giants that we face.

Paul suffered because He was determined to advance the gospel of Jesus Christ to the gentile world. He fought so that we may be partakers of the life that is life indeed. So everything he faced was purpose oriented – the beatings, imprisonments – but he still chose to rejoice.

In Acts 16, he and Silas were thrown in prison because Paul had rebuked a fortune telling demon out of a young girl. Her owners became angry because they had lost their means of making money and had him and Silas incarcerated. Paul was fulfilling his role and was thrown in prison for doing the right thing. This would have been a good time to complain or become defiant. But what did he choose? He and Silas chose to celebrate, so much so that God moved miraculously on their behalf when the jail was shaken and they became free men. Celebration in the midst of chaos can change the outcome of our situation and free us from our chains. I encourage you to try it!

Paul imposed the Kingdom of God every place he went. He didn't tip toe around trying to get the message out, but He declared "Jesus is Lord" everywhere he went and taught about the life giving power of the Blood of Jesus.

> And from the days of John the Baptist until now the kingdom of heaven suffers violence, and the violent take it by force.
>
> (Matthew 11:12 NKJV)

We have to make up our minds that no matter what happens, we are going to fight to the finish and take it by force. There is no time left for playing church because "our salvation is nearer now than when we first believed" (Romans 13:11). But we who comprise the church have to rise up and advance this gospel. It may not be pretty, easy or comfortable, but we must be determined to impose this life-giving Kingdom.

What gets us through the rough times? It is choosing to celebrate, praying and praising in all situations and, meditating on the Word of God daily – all of these practices will help us to press through. But we need to do more than just meditate on the Word of God. We also have to become intimately acquainted with the God of the Word, by spending time in His presence.

We need to make it a regular practice of reacquainting and reconnecting ourselves with the God we serve.

Who is the God you serve!

He is the God of Abraham, who heard God's call to leave everything; who received his miracle child at the age of one hundred and then was willing to sacrifice his son at God's command.

He is the God of Isaac, who sowed in the middle of a famine and received a hundredfold blessing.

He is the God of Jacob, who in desperation wrestled with God all night for a blessing, so much so that he came away with a new and powerful name: Israel, which means "triumphant with God, who prevails with God."

He is the God of Noah, who heard God's voice to build the ark and did so in obedience despite the teasing and ridicule, and as a result he and his family were saved from the flood that destroyed the whole world.

He is the God of Moses, who heard God's call in a burning bush and bombarded Pharaoh's ear with the command of God to let His people go; who lifted up his staff and the Red Sea was parted and stood up on either side for God's people to go through safely on dry land.

He is the God of Joshua, who led the Israelites with the command to take the city of Jericho by walking around it for seven days; and on the seventh day, the seventh time around, they shouted and the walls came tumbling down and they possessed their promise.

He is the God of Daniel, who refused to follow the king's order not to pray, but as was his custom knelt before an open window and prayed to his God; who because of this had to spend the night in a den filled with hungry lions, and was able to sleep in peace… unharmed.

He is the God of Shadrach, Meshach and Abednego, who refused to bow down to a statue made by man, but were found still standing and holding their position of allegiance to the God above all gods. They were thrown in the fiery furnace and God showed up in the midst of the furnace and these three Hebrew boys came out of that furnace unharmed and unscathed, with not even the smell of fire on their clothes and as a result were promoted.

He is the God of Peter, who decided to come out of the boat of comfort and walk on the water on the command of Jesus to come. Peter spent 40 days in that upper room and came out baptized in the Holy Ghost of God, preaching the sermon of his life that led to the salvation of 3,000 souls.

He is the God of Paul, the persecutor who became the persecuted. He was beaten, imprisoned, lied about, ambushed, shipwrecked, all in an ardent push to get this gospel of Jesus Christ throughout the world in his time. Paul wrote two-thirds of the New Testament – words that we look to for comfort and strength today. We have those words today because Paul didn't give up but pressed, overcame and finished.

All these persons walked with God and talked with God. God knew them and they knew God in a personal way. Their lives displayed God's miracle working power and have become a testimony to all generations that the God we serve is omnipotent (all powerful), omnipresent (everywhere) and omniscient (all knowing).

God is the same yesterday, today and forever. Therefore, He is the God Who empowers us to press, overcome and finish as well! He will fight our battles and win, just like He did for them thousands of years ago.

Know the God of the Word

We can never really believe the Word of God, until we really know the God of the Word. When we know the God of the Word, then the Word of God becomes believable and meaningful to us. We will then have the faith that causes us to overcome and finish because we are assured of God's presence, power and protection. It's not that God has changed, but our faith level has increased because we trust Who we know. The more time we spend getting to know God, the more secure we will feel, because we know the power of the God we serve.

> You who sit down in the High God's presence, spend the night in Shaddai's shadow, Say this: "GOD, you're my refuge. I trust in you and I'm safe!" (Psalm 91:1-2 MSG)

At the end of this psalm, God tells us who He will protect: "'If you hold on to me for dear life', says God, 'I will get you out of any trouble. I'll give you the best care, if you'll only get to know and trust Me. Call Me and I'll answer, be at your side in bad times; I'll rescue you, then throw you a party! I'll give you a long life, give you a long drink of salvation!'"

Press on!

Let's determine to fight to the finish because people out there are dying and their deliverance is wrapped up in our purpose. Let's not give up. Paul encourages us:

> So we're not giving up. How could we! Even though on the outside it often looks like things are falling apart on us, on the inside, where God is making new life, not a day goes by without his unfolding grace. These hard times are small potatoes compared to the coming good times, the lavish celebration prepared for us. There's far more here than meets the eye. The things we see now are here today, gone tomorrow. But the things we can't see now will last forever.
> (2 Corinthians 4:16-18 MSG)

I have been saved for over 20 years and found that I have grown and developed the most spiritually in the hard times and during the trials. There have been some painful situations I have had to endure including being raped, but I have determined to overcome and finish. I still have joy!

Like Paul, let's celebrate because God has given us the power to finish what has been started in us. Let's celebrate because we have a God Who is bigger than any obstacle we face. Let's choose to celebrate because our God "is able to do exceeding abundantly above all that we ask or think, according to the power that worketh in us!" (Ephesians 3:20)

11

CHAPTER

STAY STEADFAST

*I*n order to be a runner who endures to the end, we must realize that it does not matter what hand we were dealt at the outset of the race, but what we do with that hand that will determine the outcome in the race of our lives. Many people have come from humble and challenging beginnings, but they did not allow those challenges to deter them, but propel them to accomplish their goals, fulfill their God-given purpose and impact the lives of many other runners around them. Their stories should truly motivate us to be the best God intends for us to be, no matter what setbacks we may experience.

I am always amazed how God teaches me some valuable life lessons through movies and television programs. I was deeply moved and encouraged when I watched the movie *The Pursuit of Happyness*[1]. This film starred Will Smith and told of the real life story of Chris Gardner. The movie expounds on the story of an impoverished but brilliant young man, who found himself abandoned by his girlfriend and was forced to care for his young son.

Life was tough for Gardner and his son and they were subjected to homelessness, unemployment and uncertainty. There were many low times in his life, but Gardner was determined to succeed. To him, every day presented a new opportunity to press towards his dream, no matter what the previous day had dealt him. He even accepted an unpaid intern job at the prestigious Dean Witter investment firm at a time when he needed money the most. Only one intern would be chosen for a permanent job after the program. Despite the obstacles that he faced, Gardner learned to overcome each one and at the end of the program, he was the one chosen for the permanent position.

What was it that this young man possessed that caused him to stay in the game even with two runners out and two strikes against him? It was determination and perseverance.

In life, there are going to be many challenges that we must face as we run our race, but in order to succeed and be all God has called us to be and do all that God as called us to do, we have to be determined and we have to persevere.

Things are not going to be the same all the time. Sometimes, all will be calm and there are times when storms will rage. The key to success is to learn how to stay steadfast though it all. Will our belief systems, faith, countenance and composure rise and fall with the circumstances of life? Or will we remain fully convinced that "He who began a good work in us, will carry it on to completion until the day of Jesus Christ?"

> There has never been the slightest doubt in my mind that the God who started this great work in you would keep at it and bring it to a flourishing finish on the very day that Christ Jesus appears.
>
> (Philippians 1:6 MSG)

If God has made this commitment to us to finish what He started, then what keeps us from getting to His destination for our lives? The answer to this question lies with us, not God. *We* get discouraged; *we* get depressed; *we* let go and *we* give up. The only way to pursue our passions and finish our course is to stay steadfast.

> Therefore, my beloved, be ye steadfast, unmovable, always abounding in the work of the Lord, forasmuch as ye know that your labor is not in vain in the Lord. (1 Corinthians 15:58)

We are encouraged to remain steadfast. Yes everything may not always be great; yes things change, but God never changes and our faith in Him should not change with circumstances. If we believe in God, we can stay steadfast, endure and finish our course.

I believe that there are three keys to staying steadfast in pursuit of our God-given dream:

Put your hope in God

> Why, my soul, are you downcast? Why so disturbed within me? Put your hope in God, for I will yet praise Him, my Savior and my God.
> (Psalm 42:5 NIV)

To put your hope in God is to realize that no matter what is going on in our lives, God is in control and has the ultimate say. God has the answers. If we could just remain composed, prayerful, joyful and at peace, we can outlast any problem or setback no matter how big or small. That is why we should be able to command our souls to give God a "yet praise". We know that in the end there is a place of victory for us in Christ Jesus. He is the Alpha and Omega. He was the establisher of our beginning and He has already been in our end and declared victory. It's just a matter of time before we get there.

How do we put our hope in God? I believe this is how we do it:

> I remember my affliction and my wandering, the bitterness and the gall. I well remember them and my soul is downcast within me. Yet this I call to mind and therefore I have hope: Because of the Lord's great love (mercy) we are not consumed, for his compassions never fail. They are new every morning; great is your faithfulness. I say to myself, 'The Lord is my portion; therefore I will wait for Him'.
>
> (Lamentations 3:19-24 NIV)

We have to ask ourselves is the Lord our portion? Hoping in God means remembering that it is God's mercy that is keeping us, step by step. His mercy is new with each day break. There is a continual supply

15

that never runs out. That is why we can put our hope in God!

In the movie, Gardner put his hope in the dream of being a stockbroker. He saw a man driving a Ferrari and asked him what he did for a living. The man told him he was a stockbroker and as a result Gardner determined that no matter what, he was going to become a stock broker as well. Seeing what that man had accomplished kept him going. We as children of the Most High God can put our hope in the giver of our dreams and the One Who has called us to this race – God Himself – and know that by His grace and mercy, we will reach His desired end for our lives: we will live in the dream and finish our course.

Pause for a "Be still and know that I am God" moment

God is our refuge and strength, an ever present help in trouble. Therefore we will not fear, though the earth gives way and the mountains fall into the heart of the sea, though its waters roar and foam and the mountains quake with their surging. (Psalm 46:1-3 NIV)

How can we not fear and stay steadfast in the midst of this kind of turmoil? I believe verse 10 of this psalm is the key.

Be still and know that I AM GOD. I will be exalted among the nations, I will be exalted in the earth. (Psalm 46:10 NIV)

There are times in life when everything seems to be falling apart. If we watch the evening news, there always seems to be more bad news than good nowadays – tornadoes, hurricanes, school shootings, plane crashes. There just seems to be the general sense of hopelessness, worldwide. Sometimes, it feels like the earth itself is giving way.

In the movie, Gardner reached his breaking point when homeless, he and his son were forced to spend the night locked in a filthy restroom, because they arrived at the shelter too late and there was no more room. It really seemed like all hope was gone and Chris began to weep in agony, not knowing how to face another day.

When we reach our breaking point, this is the time to stop, throw our arms up into the air and be still and know that God is God. We can cry out and say, "God, the situation doesn't look good right now, but You are good all the time and I trust You, my ever present help and strength". Then and only then will we come to the point of total surrender. We have to exalt God above the situations we face. He says He will be exalted above everything. Are we exalting the challenges we face, or are we exalting our God, the King of all kings and the Lord of all lords above everything?

This can only happen if we really know who God is – not head knowledge of Him, but heart knowledge. We need to remember all the things He has already done for us, and recall all of the benefits He has made available to us.

> O my soul, Bless God. From head to toe, I'll bless His holy name. O my soul, bless God, don't forget a single blessing! He forgives your sins – every one. He heals your diseases – every one. He redeems you from hell – saves your life! He crowns you with love and mercy – a paradise crown. He wraps you in goodness – beauty eternal. He renews your youth – you're always young in his presence. God makes everything turn out right; he puts victims back on their feet. (Psalm 103:1-6 MSG)

When we meditate on God and what He has promised to do and already done for us, this should give us an injection of faith that causes us to stay steadfast and immovable. We can stand in the face of fear because we are planted on the Rock of our salvation that cannot be moved or shaken. King David reminds us that...

> The Lord is my light and my salvation, whom shall I fear? The Lord is the stronghold of my life - of whom shall I be afraid? (Psalm 27:1 NIV)

When life hands you a lemon, make lemonade

Gardner got arrested for unpaid parking tickets the night before he was scheduled to interview with the investment firm of Dean Witter.

17

When he was released the next morning, he only had time to rush straight to the interview, dirty and shirtless. When questioned about his appearance he made jokes about it. He wasn't properly dressed but he still showed up. Life had handed him a lemon, but he chose to make lemonade. And he got the job, because of his determination, steadfastness and his unwillingness to give up.

How many of us would have still showed up for that interview? Many times we allow circumstances to keep us from getting to the place where God has prepared for us – the dream that He has destined for us to live in. All because of a small lemon!

There are others who have turned the lemon they were handed in their lives into the sweet, refreshing taste of lemonade.

I am always inspired by the stories of other runners in this race of life. This world is full of people who were dealt some lemons and instead of giving up and throwing in the towel, they pressed and accomplished great things. Helen Keller was one such person. She became blind and deaf at 19 months old as a result of an illness. Despite these setbacks (lemons), her parents sacrificed to ensure that she was educated. She became the first blind/deaf person to receive a bachelor's degree and went on to become a lecturer, author and political activist who fought for the rights of disabled people. Her life is a testimony that we can triumph over any tragedy and fulfill our destiny if we chose to allow our challenges to propel us to that place.

In my all-time favorite T.V. show, *Monk*[2], the main character Adrian Monk was also dealt some lemons. First, he was diagnosed with Obsessive Compulsive Behavior (OCD), which meant he had many phobias, such as fear of germs and heights. OCD also caused him to have to have everything in order and everything had to be perfect. Yes, many would say that this lemon crippled him, but if you looked closely, you would see that this made him the best detective in the world. His need to have everything in order allowed him to detect anything that was out of order, things that the other detectives missed, often clues essential to solving the case. He used this lemon to make lemonade.

The second lemon he was handed was his wife being killed by a car bomb. This severely crippled him. However, in the end it made him more focused. He was determined to bring his wife's killer to justice. However, not only his wife's killer, but also every other killer out there he could find along the way. People laughed at his idiosyncrasies and unconventional ways of doing things, but he always got his man or woman. He chose to make lemonade.

Almost twenty years ago, I found myself in an unfortunate situation. I was abducted, blindfolded, thrown into the trunk of car and raped by three men. After this, they tried to dispose of me by forcing me to plunge into a canal, shooting at me twice and leaving me for dead. However, God delivered from their hands alive, safe and well. As a result, I began to declare the goodness of God to all who would listen. I had many speaking engagements where I told of the miracle God had performed in my life, and I chose to focus not on the negative events but rather on God's saving power. My book, *A Time to Heal: Restoration from the Ravages of Rape*[3], was published as a testimony of God's faithfulness in my life. I wanted to give others who had been violated the hope that God had given me as he delivered me from the pain of this trauma. Recently, my husband and I traveled to Washington, D.C. to celebrate and be honored for the fact that my book was chosen to be a part of the permanent collection of the prestigious Library of Congress. Life had also handed me a lemon and I was determined to make lemonade.

We need to realize that God has some people lined up in our destiny, people who He has chosen for our lives and our stories to impact. It all depends on what we do with the lemons we are handed. Will we look at them and decide this is too much to handle and watch our lemons lose their uselessness? Or will we reflect on all the good things God has already done, mix it with the sour of the lemon and let God add His own supply of fresh, living water to make some lemonade not just for us, but also for the others whom He has chosen to benefit from our "not so good" experiences?

> And we know that in all things God works for the good of those who love him, who have been called according to his purpose.
>
> (Romans 8:28 NIV)

Remember that a lemon, like any other fruit, has a shelf life. It is only good for use for a limited time. Let's not waste our lemons. Let's be ministry minded and think about others who are waiting on our lemonade.

As we wrap up this chapter, let's determine to stay steadfast and remember:

Whose battle it is

2 Chronicles 20 tells us all about Jehoshaphat and the people of Israel's encounter with the armies of Moab, Ammon and Mount Seir who were planning an all-out attack on them. After prayer and fasting, the prophetic Word of the Lord came forth that the battle was not theirs, but God Himself was going to fight against their enemies.

> Don't be afraid; don't pay any mind to this vandal horde. This is God's war, not yours. (2 Chronicles 20:15 MSG)

Our battle is God's and there hasn't been one battle that He has not won.

We are to take our positions and stand!

Verse 17 of the same chapter says, "You won't have to lift a hand in this battle; just stand firm, Judah and Jerusalem and watch God's saving work for you take shape. Don't be afraid, don't waiver. March out boldly tomorrow – God is with you." Just like Jehoshaphat and Israel, we are to follow God's directives to march, take our positions and stand firm. Then, we will see the mighty rescue operation God will work on our behalf, as we stay steadfast.

Those who wait upon the Lord shall renew their strength

He energizes those who get tired, and gives fresh strength to dropouts. For even young people tire and drop out, young folk in their prime stumble and fall. But those who wait upon God get fresh strength. They spread their wings and soar like eagles, they run and don't get tired, they walk and don't lag behind. (Isaiah 40:29-31 MSG)

When we depend on God's strength, we will be restored and can continue on our course in our pursuit of our dream. Waiting on God is more than lying prostrate before Him. It is actually a lifestyle of serving Him, in the same way a waiter serves us in a restaurant. It is not passive but active. In serving God where He calls us, we are being strengthened as we continue steadfastly towards our goal. When we wait on God, we are guaranteed His power. Who is your power source? Is it God or something else?

I am reminded of the childhood story of the tortoise and the hare that both began a race. The hare started off with a bang but soon fell asleep, overconfident of victory. The tortoise began and continued slowly and steadily, never stopping. He soon passed the sleeping hare and went on to a surprising victory. His words at the end are an encouragement to us – "slow and steady, wins the race".

In real life, it did not end for Gardner at Dean Witter, as he went on to establish his own brokerage firm, Gardner Rich. Chris Gardner became a multi-millionaire who has not forgotten the challenges he faced. He gives back to many charitable organizations to empower homeless inner city people. He used his lemon well and now thousands are benefitting from his lemonade. Gardner may not have started fast, but he is sure finishing strong! This shows us how steadfastness pays off.

What about us? Will we remain steadfast? Paul admonished the Corinthians to therefore be steadfast. If we look a few verses above we will understand why:

Listen, I tell you a mystery: We will not all sleep, but we shall all be changed – in a flash, in the twinkling of an eye, at the last trumpet. For

21

the trumpet shall sound, the dead will be raised imperishable, and we will all be changed. (1 Corinthians 15:51-52 NIV)

Won't it all be worth it – staying steadfast and pressing through – when the trumpet sounds and we are all changed? I encourage you to keep moving towards the dream that God has given you; keep running your race. The key to staying steadfast is knowing that Jesus is in the boat with us and He will see us safely over to the over side… no matter what storms arise.

Have faith in God!

CHAPTER 3

SLAY THE GIANT

*I*f we are to overcome the obstacles we face as we fight to reach the finish line in this race of our lives, we need to learn how to slay the giants that have erected themselves in our lives. In this context, a giant is something or someone that stands in our way, intimidating us from moving forward into the things that God has called us to do. It stands tall and every time we attempt to move forward, it rears its ugly head, hurls insults at us and tries to convince us that we will be defeated if we go ahead.

Sadly, many times, as Christians, we live in the doldrums of doubt and despair allowing the enemy to steal our joy, peace and hope, telling us that we cannot do the things God has called us to do. And for far too long, we have allowed fear to push out faith, doubt to still our shout, and tragedy to crush our trust in God and His Omnipresence, Omnipotence and Omniscience.

It is time for us to remember who we are and Whose we are and that God said that we are more than conquerors through Christ Jesus (Romans 8:37). God has said in Psalm 84:11 "no good thing He will withhold from them that walk uprightly." He has also assured us in 2 Timothy 1:7 that "He has not given us a spirit of fear, but of power, love and of a sound mind". So in God we are fearless! However, in life we sometimes allow things, other people or circumstances to convince us that we are not. These giants come to get us to surrender and not fight to the finish. If we give in, then the enemy has us right where he wants us.

What are some of the situations we face that distract us from fulfilling our purpose? It could be something outward, such as financial trouble, a debilitating disease, a sick or wayward child, a frustrating job, a failing marriage, or family discord. It could also be something internal, such as a negative attitude, low self-esteem, jealousy, a callous or uncaring spirit, a secret sin or pride. Whatever it is, it keeps us grounded and we are unable to "mount up on wings like eagles" and soar into our destiny. These things try to keep us stagnant in our Christian race, because every morning when we arise they are there to hurl their insults at us, and likewise every night, when we lay our heads on our pillows these are the last things we think about before we fall asleep. Therefore we have remained unable to soar.

But whatever it is, God says, "we are to stand our ground, and after we have done everything, to stand" (Ephesians 6:13 NIV). God has given us some weapons to use to completely slay the giants we face, annihilate them and reclaim territory for Jesus Christ! Remember "… greater is He that is in you, that he that is in the world" (1 John 4:4). We have the power through the Blood of Jesus Christ and He has already assured us that He will fight our battles.

Who is this uncircumcised Philistine?

I am reminded of the story of David and Goliath that is recorded in 1 Samuel 17. Israel, God's chosen people, was also facing a giant. They were at war with the Philistines in Judah. The Philistine army had a champion named Goliath who was nearly ten feet tall, dressed in heavy bronze armor and had been a warrior from his youth. In other words, he looked invincible and like a winner before the battle even started.

The Israelites, on the other hand, did not have a suitable contender to face this giant of a man. What made it worse was that Goliath knew this, so he taunted the army of Israel and hurled insults at them every morning. He would say:

> Why bother using your whole army? Am I not a Philistine enough for you? And you're all committed to Saul, aren't you? So pick your best fighter and pit him against me. If he gets the upper hand and kills me, the Philistines will all become your slaves. But if I get the upper hand and kill him, you'll all become our slaves and serve us. I challenge the troops of Israel this day. Give me a man. Let us fight it out together!

(1 Samuel 17:8-10 MSG)

In the natural, no one in his right mind from the Israelite army would even consider fighting a ten-foot tall man on his own. So their response was to cower in fear.

Meanwhile, David was sent by his father Jesse to take supplies to his brothers who were soldiers in the Israelite army. David arrived just in time to hear Goliath hurl his threats at Israel. He was not a fighting man like his three older brothers. All of his life, David had been a shepherd, tending his father's sheep. He would have been the most unlikely individual to slay the giant. But David had courage and he was not afraid. He knew Who he served, the Almighty God, and he refused to remain silent when threatened. While the soldiers were looking with their physical eyes at how they were going to be defeated, David saw with spiritual eyes how small Goliath was in light of the mighty God he served. He responded in verse 26 with righteous indignation, "Who is this uncircumcised Philistine that he should defy the armies of the living God?"

> ### Be courageous and face your giants

The uncircumcised Philistine in our lives is the thing that stands in our way, hurling threats at us as we run our course, all in an attempt to get us to give up!

As Christians, David's response should be the cry of our hearts as well when we face giants in our lives that try to intimidate us. We should not shrink back in fear because of Who lives on the inside of us, the King of Kings and the Lord of lords, the all-conquering Lion of the Tribe of Judah – Jesus Christ Himself! We need not fear or be afraid because of "Christ in us, the hope of glory."

The story of David and Goliath so often mirrors our lives as Christians. 1 Samuel 17:16 tells us "for forty days the Philistine came forward every morning and evening and took his stand." Many times we face what seems to be insurmountable circumstances in our lives and we become paralyzed with fear and alarm. Will God show up for us in this, we often ask. But the truth is that God promises "never to leave or forsake us" in Hebrews 13:5, and so He is always with us, in the good and the bad. Every morning and evening, we may still see our adversary coming before us to take its stand, but we know that we have Someone bigger and better on our side! Therefore, we can rejoice, because we know that it is just a matter of time before we receive our breakthrough.

The Word of God says in Exodus 14:13, "the Egyptians you see today you will never see again." The Israelites were slaves to the Egyptians for four hundred years. Imagine that! However, when God was ready to deliver them, He moved mightily with signs and wonders, even parting the Red Sea to allow them to cross as on dry land. But when their adversaries tried to access that provision, they were drowned. God is bringing us to the place where we will walk in what others drown in, all because we are His and we are determined not to throw in the towel, but fight to reach the finish line. We have to become firm in our resolve like David, and not be moved by the size, "splendor" and magnitude of the giants we face.

Remember, Samuel had already anointed David as the next king of Israel in 1 Samuel 16:13. Dealing with the uncircumcised Philistine was a part of the process David had to go through, to be able to handle all of the challenges and battles he would face as the King of Israel. When David faced future battles as King, all he needed to remember was that God caused him to be successful with Goliath, so he knew that God would give him success and victory as he led His chosen people.

It is the same with us. As we run this race of our lives, we must remember the past faithfulness of God and the victories He has already won for us. This will give us the faith to believe and the motivation to keep going forward. David had proven God even before Goliath. While he was taking care of his father's sheep, he was approached by lions and bears. He had to learn how to depend on God to defeat them. He destroyed them by the power of Almighty God and so he knew that God would give Goliath over to him as well. We, as Christians, also have all of the power of Almighty God backing us. Therefore, we can…

> Be strong in the Lord and in his mighty power. Put on the full armor of God so that you can take your stand against the devil's schemes
>
> (Ephesians 6:10-11 NIV)

The Message Bible really breaks it down for us so that we can understand how to use the full armor of God to protect us.

> And that about wraps it up. God is strong and He wants you strong. So take everything the Master has set out for you, well-made weapons of the best materials. And put them to use so that you will be able to stand up to everything the Devil throws your way. This is no afternoon athletic contest that we'll walk away from and forget about in a couple of hours. This is for keeps, a life-or-death fight to the finish against the Devil and all his angels. Be prepared. You're up against more than you can handle on your own. Take all the help you can get, every weapon God has issued, so that when it's all over but the shouting, you'll still be on your feet. Truth, righteousness, peace, faith, and salvation are more than just words. Learn how to apply them. You'll need them throughout your life. God's Word is an indispensable weapon. In the same way, prayer is essential in this ongoing warfare. Pray hard and long. Pray for your brothers and sisters. Keep your eyes open. Keep each other's spirits up so that no one falls behind or drops out
>
> (Ephesians 6:10-18 MSG)

This is powerful. God has provided us with all we need to overcome the obstacles we face as we fight to the finish line. He has already warned us that it won't be easy, but ultimate victory is ours and we will still be on our feet when it is all over. He has given us some weapons – truth, righteousness, peace, faith, salvation, His Word and prayer – but we have to learn how to use them properly. We should always speak the truth in love and be in right standing with God through the Blood of Jesus Christ.

God's peace surpasses all human understanding and guards our hearts and minds. We know that He is sovereign and everything will work out for our good. So, we can rest in the peace of God. Faith in God and His Word is key because we can read God's Word, take Him at it and believe that if "He said it, He will bring it to pass" (Numbers 23:19). Therefore, no matter what the enemy is saying or how big the giant may appear, we can have faith in God and His ability to give us the victory.

We can also depend on God's saving power (salvation), that on the cross Jesus paid it all for us and there is blessing, protection, provision, deliverance, healing, peace, and rest made available to us through the Blood of Jesus Christ.

We have the Word of God (the Sword of the Spirit) that we can remind God of and when we pray, we pray His Word back to Him. This is the Word that "He honors above all His Name". He has said, "Heaven and earth will pass away, but My Word will never pass away." God's sword in our mouths will demolish the enemy's lies in our minds and schemes in our lives when we open our mouths and declare the Word of God over our situations. Paul, in this passage, encourages us to pray hard and long and not just to pray for ourselves, but for all God's people so that no one will be left behind in this race or now one will give up and drop out. We are our brother's keeper and it is our responsibility to watch out for them and hold onto them, even if we have to drag them across the finish line with us.

We have been anointed by God so let's be bold and go out to face and defeat the giants that present themselves to us as we run this race of life. The back of the adversary must be broken and it is God Who is giving us the victory this very day.

How David triumphed over the giant

Let's examine how David triumphed over Goliath. David told Saul not to fear because he would fight the giant for him. Saul did not believe David would be successful but he was out of options. So, he gave David his armor and wished him luck. Saul's armor was too big and heavy for David. He quickly recognized that if he was going to slay the giant, he would have to do it God's way. David remembered how God had been training him all his life when he faced the smaller giants. So David took out his slingshot and collected five smooth stones and approached the giant. When Goliath laughed at and cursed him, David had just had about enough. This was his reply:

> "You come at me with sword and spear and battle-ax. I come at you in the name of God-of-the-Angel-Armies, the God of Israel's troops, whom you curse and mock. This very day God is handing you over to me. I'm about to kill you, cut off your head, and serve up your body and the bodies of your Philistine buddies to the crows and coyotes. The whole earth will know that there's an extraordinary God in Israel. And everyone gathered here will learn that God doesn't save by means of sword or swear. The battle belongs to God – He's handing you to us on a platter." (1 Samuel 17:44-47 MSG)

David had so much faith in God's ability to act and back him that he gave God the credit for the victory before the battle even began. He remembered God's faithfulness and His manifested power in the past, and was willing to step out in faith again against the biggest enemy he had to face thus far. He acknowledged that it was God Who was handing Goliath over to them. He just had to do what God instructed, and God would do the rest to give him and the Israelites victory. David began to magnify the Lord, in the midst to the battle, by saying that after this battle was fought, everyone would know and recognize that there is an extraordinary God in Israel. In essence, he was saying, "After today, you won't mess with us when you see how big our God is."

After making this statement, David charged forward, slung his shot and hit the giant right in the middle of his forehead and killed him. David did not stop there; he finished him off by cutting his head off just like he said he would. And that was the end of Goliath, the giant who had insulted, cursed and intimidated Israel for forty days. One move of God by a man of faith and he was gone.

The best part about this story, though, was the fact that all of the other Philistine soldiers who were hiding behind Goliath's strength, fled when they realized that their champion was gone. So Israel recognized that they were just as afraid and they pursued the remaining Philistines until they were all dead. The strongman had been defeated, and all the other imps that got their strength and courage from the strongman ran in fear.

If we will have faith in God like David did, and be courageous enough to face the giants in our lives like fear, worry, sickness, lack, confusion, discord and others then God will give these vices into our hands and we can cut off their heads for good. Then all the little imps hanging around them will flee in fear when they see how big our God is! God then instructs us to pursue them until they are completely destroyed so that we can continue to run our race with patience. How do we face the giants? We confront them with the Word of God!

The blessings of taking a stand

God blessed David immeasurably for taking a stand against Goliath. He received from Saul great wealth (increase), his daughter's hand in marriage (intimacy) and exemption from taxes (immeasurable favor). In the same way, if we take God at His Word and take a stand for righteousness against the giants we face, God will supernaturally bless us as well. There is a blessing that comes from obedience. We will experience increase, intimacy, and immeasurable favor like David did.

However, these will not come without opposition. Even in just considering to step out in faith on God's Word and face our giants, there may be many who oppose us because in being courageous, we expose other people's weaknesses or unwillingness to do so. Those who will oppose us are generally very close to us: friends, church members, and even our own family members. David faced opposition from his own brothers. They were jealous because David was bold enough to do in one day what they had refused to do in forty.

Nobody thought that David could slay the giant, because they looked at the natural circumstances. If we focus on what we see, we will be defeated. We focus again on a scripture we used in the previous chapter.

> So we're not giving up. How could we! Even though on the outside it often looks like things are falling apart on us, on the inside, where God is making new life, not a day goes by without His unfolding grace. These hard times are small potatoes compared to the coming good times, lavish celebration prepared for us. There's far more here than meets the eye. The things we see now are here today, gone tomorrow. But the things we can't see now will last forever.
>
> (2 Corinthians 4:16-18 MSG)

What an assurance! The things we see and face today, the giants of fear, sickness, lack and despair may be here today, but tomorrow they will be replaced by the things we cannot see right now: faith, hope, peace, continual provision and victory. We ought to praise God now in advance for what He has already promised us we will see and enjoy, the things that will last forever!

David had already experienced God's faithfulness and protection. So when Goliath came with all of his so called splendor and size and cursed David by his gods, David reflected on God's past victories in his life, and with one stone and a slingshot backed by the power of God, he slew him and the giant fell.

31

God has already broken the back of some of the smaller giants we have faced in the past, so like David we must remember God's past faithfulness to us and remember He's the same yesterday, today and forever. All we have to do is stand on the Word of God and believe, no matter what we see in front of us and watch God give us the victory. This is easier said than done. Nevertheless, sometimes we have to do it, even if we do it afraid. That is what courage is; it's taking action by moving forward in spite of fear or difficulties!

Let's be determined to stand and watch God give us the victory over every giant we face as we run this race.

CHAPTER 4

THE POWER OF PRAYER

*O*ne thing we need to remember as Christians is that we have one of the most powerful tools at our disposal, which we rarely use to its full potential. We carry this tool with us day after day, but it is often left unused or underused and tucked away in our back pockets and is pulled out generally in extreme circumstances or as a last resort.

If we would only realize that this tool that God has given us is the key that opens many of the doors that God has placed before us, the solution to many of our problems and the beacon that guides us into our destiny.

Of course, I am talking about prayer.

> Therefore confess your sins to each other and pray for each other so that you may be healed. The prayer of a righteous person is powerful and effective. (James 5:16 NIV)

What is prayer? Prayer is simply talking to God – us speaking to Him and Him speaking to us. If prayer is to be effective – and what God intended for it to be in our lives – we have to be in right relationship with God. Let's face it; we don't have regular conversations with people we don't have a relationship with. We don't share our thoughts, dreams and aspirations as well as our worries, concerns and fears, with just anybody. We generally share those with someone we know, someone we are in relationship with and someone we believe that we can trust. Who better than God? He has the power to turn the negative circumstances we face around for our good and take our dreams, goals and aspirations and make them a reality. Who better than our Heavenly Father – the One Who has the power to make all things work together for our good, because we love Him and are called according to His purpose? We have such an awesome gift and privilege in prayer.

Do you know we can change the world that we live in all by the way we frame our words in prayer. So many times, we just accept the way things are, sit back and live mediocre lives, and never reach our true potential. "All because we do not carry, everything to God in prayer!"

We need God every hour, no matter if things are going well or if we are experiencing difficulties. If we maintain a healthy relationship with God and a vibrant prayer life, we will be prepared for whatever life throws at us, whether good or bad. Then the bad would not be so bad for us because we would have already spent time in prayer with God, and I believe that during our prayer time He prepares us for what lies ahead.

Prayer is not just about us making our requests known to God, but it is also a time for God to speak and make His will known to us. If we believe that God has created us for and with a purpose, how will we ever know what that purpose is, if we don't spend time with Him in prayer giving Him the opportunity to share His vision for our lives with us? Sadly, many people come to planet earth filled with purpose and leave never having known why they were here or what they were to deposit on this earth.

God has given us a gift. Out of all the creatures on earth He created, God chose not to talk with the birds of the air, or the fish of the sea, but to commune with us! So let us not hide this tool on the shelf or keep it in our back pockets – but as believers in God, let us determine to utilize all that He has made available to us – especially the privilege of prayer.

I believe there are key ingredients in making prayer a powerful tool and weapon in our lives as we overcome obstacles and fight to the finish.

Powerful prayer can penetrate our prisons

Prayer can really be powerful if we would just do it. Scripture is filled with many instances where fervent prayer led to the total defeat and destruction of the enemy's plans in the lives of God's children. One such instance took place in Acts 12.

The story of Peter's miraculous escape from prison is a powerful demonstration of the effectiveness of prayer when facing obstacles. In this story, we see how Herod allowed Satan to use him in persecuting the defenders of the faith. He had the apostle James killed and because this seemed to gain him popularity with the Jews, he grabbed Peter as well, thinking that God would remain silent. Therefore, he had Peter imprisoned and was planning to publicly lynch him the next day. This was all because Herod craved popularity with man. We need to be careful that in chasing after the praise of man, we don't come up against the wrath of God. I believe that this is the key verse in this chapter:

> All the time that Peter was under heavy guard in the jailhouse, the church prayed for him most strenuously. (Acts 12:5 MSG)

Peter was facing a huge obstacle, as it appeared he had been given a death sentence. After all, Herod had already had James killed and in his quest to be popular Peter death's was next on his agenda, but the church was praying.

Herod had Peter heavily guarded – shackled in chains, between two guards with two more guards posted just outside the cell. In the natural, Peter had no chance, and it seemed to be over. However, what was Peter's response? In verse 6 it said "Peter slept like a baby". What a supernatural response to a dangerous earthly situation! Peter didn't know if he would live or die the next day, but he was at peace because he knew in Whom he believed, the God Who holds tomorrow Who could "do exceedingly above all that he (we) could ever ask, or think or imagine" (Ephesians 3:20), and so he slept!

Meanwhile the church was earnestly praying and their prayers had reached the throne room of Almighty God. God sent an angel down from Heaven to the jail where Peter was. The Bible says the angel had to shake Peter out of his sleep (a man about to face certain death). What if that were us and we were facing some insurmountable challenge tomorrow, would we be able to sleep so peacefully? Or would we be up pacing the floor worrying? Would we just put it in God's hands like Peter, believe God is able and go to sleep?

> He won't let you stumble, your Guardian God won't fall asleep. Not on your life! Israel's Guardian will never doze or sleep.
>
> (Psalm 121:3-4 MSG)

So if God promises to stay up, why do we need to? God's has everything under control, and so we can rest in Him!

Let's examine how it turned out for Peter. First, the angel woke him up. Next, miraculously, his shackles fell off by themselves. He got dressed and followed the angel past the first and second guards, no problem. Then they came to an iron gate that leads outside to the city. How would they get past that? But suddenly the door just swung open, no key, no jostling, and no force. They didn't even have to touch it!

Prayer can usher in the miraculous! Prayer can open doors for us, doors we have been trying to beat down for years.

> Ask and it will be given to you; seek and you will find; knock and the door will be opened to you. (Matthew 7:7 NIV)

We, as Christians, can knock by praying.

All the time this miracle was taking place, Peter thought that he was dreaming until the angel, after walking with him for a bit, disappeared! Peter then realized he was really free! He went to the house where the prayer warriors were gathered and even though they were praying for him, they hardly expected this miraculous escape from prison, so they had a hard time believing. I don't believe that they doubted that God would save Peter, but perhaps in a more conventional way, like changing Herod's heart. But God showed that He is God all by Himself. When He heard the cry of His people in prayer, He was moved and sent His delivering agent to set His child free! It was a miracle and prayer ushered it in!

Prayer is still the answer to unlocking the miraculous today. When we face obstacles, our first response should be to pray asking God for His solution to the challenge. We can pray by ourselves or we can call upon the commitment of other believers to intercede with and for us.

Sometimes, however, we may suffer a surprise attack that may seem insurmountable and we have no opportunity to call in the "troops". What should we do in this case? When I was abducted many years ago, I did not have an opportunity to call for earthly help. Nobody knew where I was and most of the people who could help me, did not even know I had been taken captive. Thank God that I had a personal relationship with Him through Jesus Christ, and because I had called on Him many times before for the smaller things, I knew that I could count on Him yet again, in this very big trial I was facing. Without His help, I knew I was facing certain death. However, I called on God and I was saved from my enemies.

> A hostile world! I call to God. I cry to God to help me. From His palace he hears my call; my cry brings me right into his presence – a private audience! (Psalm 18:6 MSG)

In this psalm, we learn how God responds to urgent prayer:

> But me he caught – reached all the way down from sky to sea, He pulled me out of that ocean of hate, that enemy chaos, the void in which I was drowning. (Psalm 18:16-17 MSG)

The ending part of that verse always speaks volumes to my soul, because during my abduction I was disposed of in a canal. I did not know how to swim, so drowning was quite inevitable. So I can relate to David when he said that God reached down and pulled him out of "that ocean of hate". That is what He basically did when He heard the cry of the church on behalf of Peter. He ordered a mighty rescue operation and pulled him out of an ocean of hate.

No obstacle we face in too difficult for God to handle. He is all-knowing, everywhere and all-powerful, so we can depend on God to deliver us when all hope appears to be gone.

He is the One Who will deal with those who try to prevent us from getting to the finish line. Look at what happened in Peter's case. Embarrassed and infuriated, Herod had the guards executed because they could not explain what happened to Peter or where he was. It was simply a *miracle*. However, Herod's arrogance prevailed, and a short time later, God had enough. When he was giving a speech in another town and allowed the people to worship him, not giving glory to God, he collapsed right there, his body being overcome with worms!

This shows us that when our back is against the walls, God will not only part Heavens and miraculously save us, but will fight against those who have fought against us and WIN!

> Meanwhile the ministry of God's Word grew by leaps and bounds
> (Acts 12:24 MSG)

Herod's plans could not prevail against God's purpose.

Powerful prayer must be passionate

When we pray with passion, we get a hold of God's garment and cry out to God from the depths of our souls for something we have been believing Him to do. I believe our passion captures God's attention and our fervor motivates Him to act in response to our request.

In the Old Testament, Hannah is a great example of someone who prayed with passion. She was married to a man named Elkanah, who also had another wife named Peninnah. The problem for Hannah was that Peninnah had given Elkanah children, but Hannah had been unable to conceive. She was barren, so she felt unproductive, and useless. What made things worse was that Peninnah lorded this over her. She taunted Hannah because she was the one with the children. It was bad enough that Hannah felt awful about her plight, but to have someone constantly rubbing it in her face?

Have you ever been in a situation where you felt really bothered about something? You keep lamenting over the situation in your own mind, when at the same time someone comes along and just keeps taunting you about it? Well that's how Hannah felt. Her husband tried to comfort her, but she couldn't be comforted. Sometimes we look for comfort in people, but there are some things that only God can heal. Hannah wasn't looking for comfort, but she was looking for answers. She was looking for God's healing power!

While at the temple bringing her offering to God, Hannah went before the Lord and passionately cried out to Him concerning her barrenness.

> Oh, God-of-the-Angel-Armies, if you'll take a good, hard look at my pain, if you'll quit neglecting me and go into action for me by giving me a son, I'll give him completely, unreservedly to you. I'll set him apart for a life of holy discipline. (1 Samuel 1:11 MSG)

She was in such a state, silently stuttering before the Lord, that the priest, Eli, thought that she was drunk. That was just how passionate she was in pleading her case before the Lord.

We know God heard her prayer:

> Elkanah slept with Hannah his wife, and God began making the necessary arrangements in response to what she had asked. Before the year was out, Hannah had conceived and given birth to a son. She named him Samuel, explaining, "I asked God for him."
>
> (1 Samuel 1:19-20 MSG)

This should motivate us as Christians to fight to the finish and overcome every obstacle in our way. We know that God wants us to finish and to finish strong, therefore He will go into action on our behalf when we face roadblocks. As we cry out passionately to Him in prayer, God will do for us what he did for Hannah, He will begin to make the necessary arrangements in answer to our prayers!

Hannah honored her vow to the Lord, to dedicate Samuel to His service all the days of his life and left him in the temple to serve the priests. She praised as passionately as she prayed in her prayer of praise in 1 Samuel 2. God had answered Hannah's passionate prayer for sure. She had asked God for one son, but God blessed her with five more children as well. Can you say "more than enough, overflow, too much"? Hannah's passion had led to an overwhelming move of God on her behalf.

What have we been asking God for? God is motivated by our passion. He becomes passionate about what we are passionate about.

Another thing that happened for Hannah was that her rival, Peninnah, stopped teasing her, because Hannah was obviously no longer barren. In fact, she was quite productive. Passionate prayer will not only release productivity in us but will also silence the provoker in our lives.

Powerful prayer must be persistent

How many of us, when we have prayed about some obstacle we are facing always get the answer to what we are praying for immediately? Many times when we pray, it may seem like no change has taken place. So what should be our next course of action? Should we continue to pray about it or give up? I know for me there have been many times, when I have prayed and felt like nothing has changed. However, I decided to keep at it and sometimes, days, weeks, months, even years elapsed before the answer in some form or another came. It required persistence!

Jesus told his disciples and us a parable to "show us that we should always pray and not give up" (Luke 18:1). The parable was about a judge who neither feared God nor cared about man. He was constantly bombarded by a widow who wanted relief from her enemy. The judge had continually denied her claim, but this did not stop her from coming back, over and over again. She wanted relief from her enemy, so she kept asking. The judge decided that even though he wasn't obligated to assist her, her persistence would soon wear him out and so he settled her claim.

That is what persistent prayer can do for us. It can affect the changes that we are seeking. Jesus told us to pay close attention to what the unjust judge said. Then he reminded us:

> So what makes you think that God won't step in and work justice for his chosen people, who continue to cry out for help? Won't He stick up for them? I assure you, He will. He will not drag His feet. But how much of that kind of persistent faith will the Son of Man find on earth when He returns? (Luke 18:7-8 MSG)

This is a powerful statement. God is willing to do what we ask, but He is looking for people who will not give up on day one of asking, but have persistent faith in Him that He will give them relief from their enemy and the power to overcome every obstacle they face.

My family has seen the results of persistent prayer. Our youngest son had some learning challenges in his early primary school years. Once when we visited his pediatrician, he suspected that he may have had dyslexia. He also referred him to a neurologist because he was always falling down and couldn't walk on a straight line without falling. Well, we determined to pray for our son as we always had done. As a result of our prayers, God led us to move him from a large school to a smaller school environment where he would get more individual attention. He revealed that my son was just getting lost in the bigger classes and sometimes needed things explained to him again. Nothing was wrong with his brain. Since attending the smaller school, our son has consistently been on the honor roll. This year, he entered a national essay competition and was selected as the 2nd Place Winner out of over five hundred other primary school students. He is more confident and continues to excel. This is proof positive that persistent prayer pays off.

Powerful prayer must be about more than personal needs

Many times we become so occupied with our own lives that we fail to look around and see what God is concerned about. This is mostly reflected in our prayers. We often pray, "Lord, bless me. Lord I need a breakthrough. Lord help me." All these prayers are good, but if that is the extent of our prayers and we refuse to look outward and see the needs of others and this lost and dying world, then we are not praying to our full potential. Just look at the state of our world: wars, hunger, epidemics, gun violence, tornados and other deadly disasters. These things alone are enough for us to channel our prayers away from ourselves only and onto others as well. We have allowed these things to prevail, you know, because we have sat on the sidelines and done nothing about it. Where is the "real church"? Will the real church please get in a position of continual prayer?

As Christians, our job is to fall on our faces and pray for godliness to prevail in our world — on our streets, in our neighborhoods, communities, cities, and schools. Then and only then will we see the changes that we have been looking for.

In the book of Esther, we see an example of unselfish prayer. Esther was an Israelite orphan who had become Queen in a foreign land. When a plot against her people, the Jews, arose, Esther would put aside her own needs and risk her life to save her people. How did she do this? By prayer and fasting. She had to go into the king's (her husband's) presence uninvited to petition for the salvation of her people. However, if he didn't pardon her, she could lose her life. In spite of this, Esther was determined to stand in the gap for her nation.

> Go and gather together all the Jews who are in Susa, and fast for me. Do not eat or drink for three days, night and day. I, and my maids, will fast as you do. When this is done, I will go to the king, even though it is against the law. And if I perish, I perish. (Esther 4:16 NIV)

What a powerful statement of faith! Esther and the Jews fasted and prayed. She then went in to the king's presence and survived. She petitioned for the lives of her nation. The end result was this: her nation was spared and instead of the Jews being annihilated, they actually destroyed their enemies. All because, an unselfish, militant woman of God rose to the challenge and fasted and prayed with her nation for a miracle. We have a moral responsibility and obligation to make an imposition of the Kingdom of God in our world. We are the gatekeepers of the cities and we should not allow any foul and ungodly spirits to take root in our countries or the world at large. God has given us an opportunity to influence those where we live. No situation is too far-gone for God to handle. He is all-powerful and He can and will turn it around for good if we would stand in the gap and pray.

Powerful prayer will protect you

One key element to praying the kind of prayers that are powerful and effective, is praying prayers based on the Word of God. The scriptures are filled with verses that speak of the protection that God provides for His children. If we begin to meditate on the protection God offers us in His Word, then we will begin to experience His power of protection from harm and danger, from sickness and disease, from the plans of the enemy and from anything that would try to come up against us as we fight to the finish.

Reading and praying God's Word is indeed a power source. In Psalm 91:7-13, God promises that harm can't get near us. We will watch the wicked turn into corpses from a safe distance. Since God is our refuge, evil cannot get close to us, harm cannot get through the door. His angels are assigned to us to protect us and keep us from falling. We have the power over all of the lions and the snakes in our path. What a mighty God we serve! He guarantees that if we are in right relationship with Him and abiding under His shadow in constant communion with Him, we will experience His ultimate protection. Isn't God awesome?

Psalm 34:7 promises that "God's angel sets up a circle of protection around us while we pray." So even while we are yet praying, God's angel is dispatched surrounding us with a wall of protection. Verses 17-18 also provide us with another wonderful assurance, "Is anyone crying for help? God is listening, ready to rescue you. If your heart is broken, you'll find God right there. If you are kicked in the gut, He'll help you catch your breath." Again, God promises to be there for us, never leave us or forsake us and be everything we need Him to be. This shows us that we need to know God's Word to call Him in remembrance of it and watch Him show up in a mighty way for us!

Prayer will also cause us to correctly perceive God's providence and sovereignty when we are surrounded by the enemy. In 2 Kings 6:16-17, Elisha tells his servant, "'Don't be afraid... those who are with us are more that those who are with them.' And Elisha prayed, 'O Lord, open his eyes so he may see.' And then the Lord opened the servant's eyes, and he looked and saw the hills full of horses and chariots of fire all around Elisha."

Elisha's enemies had come to surround him and his servant could only see the physical army and became afraid. Being surrounded by a physical army did not affect Elisha at all, because he was a man of prayer and through his praying, he perceived that God had already surrounded him with His angelic army, which no foe could withstand. The servant couldn't see with spirit eyes. Only prayer could reveal to the servant the type of protection Elisha was packing.

Do you feel surrounded? Well, tap into the power of prayer and let God Himself reveal to you the fact that you are already surrounded and encamped about with His angels!

Here is one final question in this chapter: What if we have prayed and prayed and God says "No"? What do we do then? Not everything we pray for will get a resounding "Yes". Sometimes God will say "Not yet" and sometimes He may even say "No". The apostle Paul had such an experience where he had prayed to God about a handicap he had been given to keep him grounded because of all of the great things that God had allowed him to see. What was Paul's response to this handicap?

> Satan's angel did his best to get me down; what he in fact did was push me to my knees. No danger then of walking around high and mighty! At first I didn't think of it as a gift, and begged God to remove it.
>
> (2 Corinthians 12:7 MSG)

So, Paul's response was to pray and ask God to take it away. Wouldn't that have been our response as well? After all, who wants to deal with discomfort? I think his response was appropriate, pray first and ask God to deal with it.

What was God's response? In verse 9, it says, "My grace is enough, it's all you need. My strength comes into its own in your weakness." God replied "Yes, most times I am going to take it away, but there are some things that are not pleasant but are beneficial for your growth and development, to keep you grounded, so just depend on my grace (my supernatural enabling power) to see you through every dark day concerning this issue."

Let's be clear. This was not referring to a sin issue, because God doesn't entertain sin. Through the power of the Blood of Jesus, we can conquer sin! It would be an issue we must deal with in order to stay grounded in and connected to Christ. We deal with it by relying on the grace of God.

What should be our response, then? We should respond like Paul and say: "Once I heard that, I was glad to let it happen. I quit focusing in the handicap and began appreciating the gift. It was a case of Christ's strength moving in on my weakness. Now I take limitations in stride, and with good cheer, these limitations that cut me down to size – abuse, accidents, oppositions, bad breaks. I just let Christ take over! And so the weaker I get, the stronger I become."

It is imperative to remember Who we serve. If God brings us to it, He will bring us through it. We will either have the victory here on earth or in Heaven with Him. One thing is for sure: we will have the victory and powerful prayer will usher it in! Most times it is here on earth, but in the case with some issues, such as what Paul experienced, ultimate victory comes in Heaven with God where Satan can no longer torment us!

God has shown us in his Word and throughout our own lives, and the lives of others, that powerful things can happen when we pray – chains can fall off, barrenness can be dispelled, our claims can be addressed, nations can be saved and delivered, and our weaknesses can be turned into strengths!

In the final episode of the television show, *Monk*, Adrian Monk at the lowest point of his life is found holding a beautifully wrapped Christmas gift that his wife left behind for him, just before she was murdered. For twelve years, he had placed this box on the shelf in his living room seeing it as the last secret between them. For twelve years, he had also searched tirelessly for his wife's killer but to no avail. However, when he was at the point of death, he decided to open this gift and reveal the last secret between them. Little did he know that the answer to his wife's murder mystery was sitting in that box all that time! If only he had opened the box from day one, he could have saved himself twelve years of agony.

This was so profound to me, because God spoke to me in this episode saying that we as Christians have been left a gift by Him as well and that gift is the ability to reach His throne room anytime and anyplace through prayer. However, if we never found out what is inside that gift box, we will never really tap into the powerful access we have as children of God. There are goodies inside but we cannot benefit from them until we lay hold of them by opening the box. The answers to all our concerns are in that box! God is saying, "Get the gift off of the shelf; open the gift; it's all in the gift that I left you."

So let's not wait any longer to unwrap this gift our Heavenly Father has left for us until He returns. Let's unwrap the gift of prayer and experience the power within!

CHAPTER 5

"FEAR NOT," SAYS THE LORD

I truly believe that one of the obstacles we will face over and over again as we run this race with patience is fear. Fear is **F**alse **E**vidence **A**ppearing **R**eal. Every time we press forward and fight to the finish, the enemy will throw something in our pathways in an attempt to frighten us off of the course God has set for us so that we do not get to God's desired end for our lives.

How many times have we invested time fearing something that never actually materialized? This thing occupied our thought space for days, and we agonized over it, wondering if it would happen, when it would happen and how it would happen. Meanwhile the work of God assigned to us was left undone because we chose to become so pre-occupied with this *thing* that might happen. Then after a while, we begin to trust God and take Him at His Word and we overcome that fear of the moment and continue to run the race. Until we get to the next hurdle and there it is again, something is presented to us and that old, familiar feeling of fear and paranoia begins to surface again. "But I thought I had been delivered", you may say, but here it is again, staring you right in the face: FEAR!

What are some of the things that we fear: fear of harm, fear of sickness, fear of embarrassment, fear of exposure, fear of losing it all (job, spouse, family), and the big one, fear of death. Maybe what you are afraid of right now may not be on this list, but I am sure that at some time or another you feared one of these things. I will give you an opportunity to put your current fear in black and white.

I am battling with the fear of _____.

Write it in now! The sooner we acknowledge the fear, the sooner we can demolish it by the power of Almighty God.

When fear is out of control

I have personally experienced some battles where the spirit of fear tried to take hold of me and cripple me so that I could not reach my destiny. That is what fear does to us: it cripples and paralyzes us so that we are unable to move forward and do the good that God intends for us to do.

A few years ago I came down with a terrible flu. I became so weak and the pain and aches were unbearable. Then the fear set in because I had heard of so many people who had died from the flu, so I started to think that I might have the killer flu. Then my heart started to race, which I learned later is a natural occurrence to a virus that would disappear after the virus was gone. But the enemy kept trying to get me to believe that I had a killer flu. I became so paranoid that I started to go to the doctor every day. I was on medication and all I needed was some rest because I had been working overtime just prior to contracting the flu. My body just was depleted and needed to be restored. Eventually, I got over the flu, but I never addressed the fear that came with it. So I would occasionally feel weak and panic would set in again: "something is wrong... I am going down!"

Then a few weeks later, my husband took sick with a stomach virus and I had to rush him to the hospital. So the fear came back again. Even though I was functionally normally on the outside, inside, the paranoia was closing in. He eventually had to be hospitalized for almost a week, and I allowed the fear to become bigger and bigger. Even after he was released from the hospital and recovering well, I still allowed my heart to be filled with anxiety (a by-product of fear). As a result, I had constant heart palpitations and rising blood pressure and almost had a breakdown.

Everything settled down for a few weeks, until my one of my sons got the flu and had to be given an IV drip. So I started to worry about him. I had allowed this fear to become so large that when anything happened, I would assume the worst and I could not experience the presence and peace of God or trust Him and stand upon His Word. I knew His Word. I lived this Word for over 20 years. But, I had allowed one small seed of fear in and to almost topple what I had been meditating on for so many years.

Well everyone got better and things appeared to be normal again, until a few weeks later, when I started to feel sick again. I went to the doctor and was diagnosed with a bladder infection. Simple enough, right?

A few days later, when the pain returned, I ended up in the emergency room and after having a scan was diagnosed with another condition that wasn't life-threatening but something that had to be managed. However, I was injected with iodine during the scan and had a terrible allergic reaction that caused me to break out in hives, jerk uncontrollably and my heart to race. So what do you think came back again? You guessed it: fear… big time! The doctors got the allergy under control that night, but the heart racing never really went away.

Within less than a week, I was rushed back to the emergency room because of an extremely high pulse rate and rising blood pressure. They checked my heart and nothing was wrong with it. It was just beating extremely fast but had a normal rhythm. I was given some medication to slow the heart rate down and after a while was released with anxiety medication. I was also told that I might have had a thyroid problem as well. Well, my heart raced and raced and so I took the anxiety pills more and more and was then prescribed beta-blockers, which would slow my heart rate down.

Any time I felt a little something strange, my heart would race and I would spiral out of control. The fear would seize me and it brought with it depression so I would cry uncontrollably all the time.

The antidote to fear: LOVE

> For God hath not given us a spirit of fear; but of power, and of love and a sound mind. (2 Timothy 1:7)

Paul gave Timothy God's antidote to fear. Instead of fear, God has given us power! Luke 10:19 says that God has given us the power to "tread on serpents and scorpions and all over the power of the enemy."

> There is no fear in love. But perfect love drives out fear, because fear has to do with punishment. The one who fears is not made perfect in love. (1 John 4:18 NIV)

If God's perfect love is deep down within us, then we have no reason to fear. His love drives out the fear that He will strike us down when we make mistakes and fall. The opposite is true: God is always there, waiting to restore us! So we have nothing to fear.

> Thou wilt keep him in perfect peace, whose mind is stayed on thee: because he trusteth in thee. (Isaiah 26:3)

We are promised a sound and steadfast mind, when we trust God to protect and take care of us. The Message Bible says it like this "people with their minds set on you, you keep completely whole, steady on their feet, because they keep at it and don't quit."

With our minds fixed on God, we will finish our course! Just remembering God loves us during the times when we feel afraid should deliver us from fear's grip. If we are loved by God, the Creator and Sustainer of the Universe, what force is there that can overpower us as we run our course?

Run in the face of fear

Now while I was facing all of these challenges, God gave me the strength to still be encouraging. Every weekend at church I exhorted others to trust in God and that God would come through for them. I had speaking engagements that I had to fight to be able to make. But, thanks to God I made them and lives were changed as a result of them. Even though I was still fearful, I had to learn how to press through. The apostle Paul declared:

> We are hard-pressed on every side, but not crushed; perplexed, but not in despair; persecuted, but not abandoned, struck down, but not destroyed. (2 Corinthians 4:8-9 NIV)

This must be our declaration as well! Although, the doctors checked all of my organs and said that everything was functioning normally, I still was taking medication that I didn't need. This was all because I allowed a small seed of fear in and it began to grow with every situation I faced. It went on a rampage in my heart and started manifesting itself in my body with the various health challenges. This was an all-out attempt by the enemy to get me to abort the vision God has for my life. During this time, it was almost as if the Word of God was being choked out of my heart. I could only hold on to a few scriptures such as "I shall not die, but live to declare the glory of God" and "by Jesus' stripes, I am healed". I am so thankful that I made it!

Don't face it alone

I realized that during times of trial, it is important not to isolate ourselves but stay connected to other believers. Satan would want us to go it alone so that he could have a better chance at defeating us. However, God never intended for us to run this race alone, but have provided us with a community of runners so that we can depend on each other. There are some people who have been running alongside us consistently. They are the ones God wants us to depend on when the waves of life try to overtake us. These are the persons who will stand by us until the storm passes by.

During my time of trial, there were many who assisted. There was one friend in particular, though, who had just come out of a health trial, and was able to help counsel and pray me through. So many days when I felt like I could not make it and the feelings of anxiety tried to flood my soul, I would go by her house to hear her speak words of faith and victory until I could believe and walk in victory again for myself. She and others held the rope for me and helped me to get back up on my feet so that I could keep running.

Thank God I had the support of my husband, parents, pastors, family and friends to pray me through and support me during this difficult time. My faith was being put to the test and my mind was being bombarded with fatal thoughts. I am glad I surrounded myself with Godly influences who prayed and spoke the Word of God, constantly, over me.

Saturate yourself with the Word of God

I also listened to the Bible on my iPad, because "faith cometh by hearing and hearing by the Word of God" (Romans 10:17). One psalm that really spoke volumes to me during this time was Psalm 27. This psalm was written by King David at the time he was running for his life. It begins "The Lord is my light and my salvation – whom shall I fear? The Lord is the stronghold of my life – of whom shall I be afraid?" Finally a small light started to flicker in my soul that I had allowed to become darkened with fear. I had to remind myself of Whose I was? I belonged to God Almighty because I was washed in the precious Blood of Jesus Christ. The Lion of the Tribe of Judah was living within me and I had the victory over this and every situation. God promised in His Word that "no-one can pluck us from His hand" (John 10:28). So, I was protected all the way through.

When the psalm says, "The Lord is my light," it means that God is a revealer of all things, because light reveals. Darkness is dispelled when the light comes. The Lord exposes all the ploys of the enemy when He shows up because He is our light. Then we can clearly see the devil for who he really is, a deceiver wrapping himself in the darkness of fear in an attempt to get us to let go of our Heavenly Father's hands so that we could begin to sink in our circumstances. However, this is the time to hold on, for dear life, to God's unshakable hands and come out of the darkness of the situation and into the marvelous light of God. 1 Peter 2:9 says, "He (Jesus) called us out of darkness into His marvelous light."

God is also our salvation, that means He is the One Who will save us from all the enemy's plans to defeat us. He not only reveals to us how the devil is trying to deceive us to believe his report of failure, defeat and death but He wants us to recognize that He is our Savior and He has the power to deliver us from any and EVERY situation we face as we fight to the finish.

Psalm 27 also assures us that God is the stronghold of our lives, so we need not fear or have any cause for alarm. Thefreedictionary.com defines stronghold as "a place of survival or refuge." God declares that He is our place of survival, safety and refuge. He is our fortress or fortified wall of protection to which we can run.

> The name of the Lord is a strong tower, the righteous run into it and are safe. (Proverbs 18:10 NKJV)

David also goes on to describe the magnitude of the Lord's protection. He says that when our enemies come up against us, it is our enemies, not us, who will be doing the stumbling and falling. Their plan is to come up against us to take us out, but our big and mighty God stands between us and them and they are destroyed. I am reminded of this scripture:

> Many are the plans of a man's heart, but it is the Lord's purpose that will prevail. (Proverbs 19:21)

Man may plan our demise, but God steps in and gives us victory. That is why we can remain calm when war breaks out against us, like the psalm says, because God is on our side. He is our source of protection and safety from sickness and disease, from insults, from hidden traps and outright attacks. God has got us covered!

> What, then shall we say in response to all these things? If God is for us, who can be against us? He Who did not spare His own Son, but gave Him up for us all - how will He not also, along with Him, graciously gave us all things? (Romans 8:31 NIV)

We must recognize that God is on our side when we are in a covenant relationship with Him through Jesus Christ His Son. Therefore, if God is standing by our side, which enemy dare come to taunt or snatch us while we are in the presence of the Almighty God? He promises in Hebrews 13:5 "never to leave or forsake us." So, no matter how dark it seems on the outside, there should always be a flicker of light shining deep down in our souls because we have His assurance that He is always with us. We can declare like the writer of Hebrews in that verse "the Lord is my helper; I will not be afraid. What can mere mortals do to me?" What can sickness and disease, fear and paranoia, struggles and strife, lack and challenges do to us when God is our helper: "our refuge and a very present help in times of trouble" (Psalm 46:1).

So let us determine to always remember that when the way seems dark and the enemy tries to flood our hearts with fear and worry as we run our race, we can depend on God's love and His Word to bring us into the place that He has prepared for us. Psalm 119:105 (NIV) reminds us that "Your (God's) word is a lamp unto my feet and a light unto my path."

The hurdles we may be facing right now may make us feel like we are walking through an unending tunnel, that is dark and the way seems unsure. However, we can be assured that even in the darkest place,

God's Word will always provide us with a lamp, so that we will have enough light to see to take one more step forward. As we exercise our faith to step forward, we will begin to notice that the Word becomes a light along the pathway that we are travelling on and it will lead us right out of the tunnel into our place of destiny. No matter how difficult it may be, it is imperative for us to hold onto the Word of God.

Matthew 24:35 says that "Heaven and earth will pass away, but My (God's) Word will never pass away" (NIV). We can depend on God's Word. Isaiah 55:11 also assures us, "so is My Word that goes out of my mouth: it will not return to me empty, but it will accomplish what I desire and achieve the purpose for which I sent it" (NIV).

God is our Father and His plans for us are good.

> "For I know the plans I have for you," declares the Lord, "plans to prosper you and not to harm you, plans to give you a hope and a future." (Jeremiah 29:11 NIV)

Let's never allow the devil to make us think that it is our plight to lead a life of suffering, discouragement and defeat, because the above verse expressly states that God's plan for us is indeed good and hopeful. He has a pleasant future in store for us, but we have to press through the present pain of the moment and choose not to fear but have faith in God's ability to heal, deliver and protect us.

There is one closing scripture I believe we should internalize as we walk out of fear and into faith:

> I lift up my eyes to the mountains — where does my help come from? My help comes from the Lord, the Maker of heaven and earth. He will not let your foot slip — He who watches over you will not slumber; indeed, He who watches over Israel will neither slumber nor sleep. The Lord watches over you — the Lord is your shade at your right hand; the sun will not harm you by day, nor the moon by night. The Lord will keep you from all harm — He will watch over your life; the Lord will watch over your coming and going both now and forevermore.
>
> (Psalm 121 NIV)

In this psalm, God promises His children ultimate protection. He will not let our feet slip, we can sleep in peace because He is always watching over us and promises not to fall asleep on us and leave us unprotected. He is continually watching over our lives, whether we are going out or coming back in. What a blessed assurance!

Get the keys

In our trials, God teaches us some principles that we need to overcome the present hurdle and continue to run our race. When we come out of the tunnel and overcome, we then possess the keys of influence in that area. Then and only then we can unlock the doors and show others, who have also been bound, the way out in their God ordained destiny.

As I began to come out the tunnel of fear, anxiety and paranoia, I determined in my mind that I was going to grab hold of those keys and lead thousands maybe even millions out, so that we may all continue to run our race for God and fight to the finish!

"Fear not, for I am with you" says the Lord!

CHAPTER 6

SPIRITUALLY FIT TO GO THE DISTANCE

*I*f we are going to be successful in running this race of our lives, we have to carefully plan a strategy for victory. Success rarely just happens, but rather it takes deliberate effort.

The mindset of a marathon runner

Marathon runners do not just wake up one morning and say, "Hey, I think I am going to run the marathon today." If they did that, they would probably not make it more than a mile or two of the twenty-six mile course. If they are serious about the race, they must establish a training program in order to build up stamina and endurance for the big race. Daily they must make the sacrifice to train, whether it is rainy or sunny, windy or calm, hot or cold and whether they feel like it or not. Success for them calls for diligence, hard work, sacrifice and effort. Also, they cannot load up on a bunch of hamburgers and hotdogs and expect to develop the lean, trim body that is needed to perform at the highest level to finish the race. They have to stick to a special diet and take many nutritional supplements. In essence, they must be physically fit.

How is it then that as Christians, running the race of our lives, we think we can be successful without proper planning and training? Nothing can be further from the truth. We must plan for success as we overcome obstacles and fight to the finish in this race of our lives. Just like planning and training for a physical race is essential, we who name the Name of Christ must plan and train to reach our respective spiritual finish lines.

When marathon runners put on their country's uniform and represent them on the world stage such as at the Olympic Games, they bring their 'A' game with the intention of finishing first and winning the prize. How much more then should we who are washed in the precious Blood of Jesus Christ, put our best foot forward and represent the King of kings and the Lord of lords with excellence? To do this, we have to offload all the spiritual junk that has been keeping us from being the best that we can be to be a mighty witness of God's greatness.

The world is watching to see how we perform. Will we continue to press when the storms of life arise during our course? Will we continue to represent our King well when the way seems dark and life uncertain or will we say enough is enough and give up? What are we made of?

Count the cost

The Christian who will continue to run the race is the one who has counted the cost and decided to get rid of all of the baggage that would weigh them down. Jesus made this clear to His disciples:

> Suppose one of you wants to build a tower. Won't you first sit down and estimate the cost to see if you have enough money to complete it? For if you lay the foundation and are not able to finish it, everyone who sees it will ridicule you, saying, 'This person began to build and wasn't able to finish.' In the same way, those of you who do not give up everything you have cannot be my disciples. (Luke 14:28-30, 33 NIV)

Let go of the unnecessary baggage

Okay so what are some of the things we need to offload in order to become lean and fit to run our race effectively? Colossians tells us that when we have made Jesus the Lord of our lives there are certain expectations of us.

> Since then, you have been raised with Christ, set your hearts on things above, where Christ is, seated at the right hand of God. Set your minds on things above, not on earthly things. For you have died, and your life is now hidden with Christ in God. (Colossians 3:1-3 NIV)

God is expecting us to take our minds off of earthy things and to focus on the Heavenly or spiritual things that are found in His Kingdom.

The next few verses actually tell us the inappropriate things that we need to get rid of in order to successfully run our race.

> Put to death, therefore, whatever belongs to your earthy nature: sexual immorality, impurity, lust, evil desires and greed, which is idolatry. Because of these, the wrath of God is coming. You used to walk in these ways, in the life you once lived. But now you must also rid yourselves of all such things as these: anger, rage, malice, slander and filthy language from your lips. Do not lie to each other, since you have taken off your old self with its practices and have put on the new self, which is being renewed in knowledge in the image of its Creator.
>
> (Colossians 3:5-10 NIV)

The Message Bible translation refers to these attitudes as "a filthy set of ill-fitting clothes". This attire will not make us spiritually fit to go the distance because it does not fit us properly. As runners, we have to be dressed in the proper clothing to compete successfully. These vices are all setbacks to the Christian life.

These attitudes and practices may come natural to us and are acceptable in society. However, in the Kingdom of God these are unacceptable and opposite to the life Jesus died to give us. Therefore, if we give in to these things, they can become weights that keep us from running the best race we can. Deciding to please society and ourselves will prevent us from becoming all that God created us to be. To us, we may feel our lives are fulfilling because we have allowed society and other people's opinions to define who we should be. However, there is so much more that God has in store for us. We are destined to be kings and queens on the earth, but so many times we settle for less, just to fit in to society's mold of what is acceptable.

I am reminded of the story of the eagle that thought he was a chicken. He was hatched with chickens and all his life he was surrounded by chickens, so he clucked, ate and flew like a chicken. In his old age, he saw a magnificent bird flying high in the sky and when he asked the chickens about that bird, he was told the bird was called the eagle, the king of the birds. Sadly, the eagle never embraced who he was because he conformed to his environment, and therefore died thinking he was a chicken all because he did not change his thinking.

What a sad story, because the eagle never became all he was destined to be – the king of the birds. What is even more of a tragedy is the fact that <u>we</u> sometimes do not live up to our full potential as God's children because we conform to our environment as well. Just like the eagle was king over those chickens and was supposed to lead and influence them, God wants us to know that we are His standard bearers that He has chosen to lead this world to live for Him.

Put on the attire that God has provided for you

If we are going to become the athlete that represents the Kingdom of God with excellence, we have to stop trying to fit into the world's mold. We did not come to fit in, but we came to take over. We can only do this if we recognize who we are and Whose we are.

> [We] are a chosen people, a royal priesthood, a holy nation, God's special possession, that [we] may declare the praises of Him who called [us] out of darkness into His wonderful light. (1 Peter 2:9 NIV)

We are privileged to be called God's special possessions who have been chosen to show the world how this race is to be run and won. When others on the sidelines see us being all God has created us to be, this will encourage them to begin their race for His honor and glory as well.

We belong to the King of kings and the Lord of lords, the Alpha and the Omega and the Beginning and the End. We should, therefore, be the trailblazers, trendsetters and pioneers as people will be looking for us to show them the way. It is time for us to "lay aside every weight" and run the race of our lives, unlocking the doors of low living and mediocrity to set the captives free!

Dressed for success

So what is the proper attire we, as Christians, should wear to run the best race possible for God?

> So, chosen by God for this new life of love, dress in the wardrobe God picked out for you: compassion, kindness, humility, quiet strength, discipline. Be even-tempered, content with second place, quick to forgive an offense. Forgive as quickly and completely as the Master forgave you. And regardless of what else you put on, wear love. It's the basic, all-purpose garment. Never be without it.
>
> (Colossians 3:12-14 MSG)

God is so awesome that He does not leave us wondering about what we should do, how we should be or what we should wear in this new life we are living for Him. He has personally picked out a wardrobe for us to clothe ourselves in each and every day of our lives. This is our dress for success. If we follow His dress code, we will be spiritually fit to run our course. Notice the attire: It is lightweight because if we are going to be effective we have to be carefree.

Compassion

Instead of being cold and callous about everything, God is saying, try on compassion for a change. We should feel for others and help them along the way as we run together for Him.

Humility

Exchange pride, which is so burdensome, for humility. Recognize that everything of value we have and will ever have comes from God. Then we don't have to worry about when things go wrong because God is the One Who provided it and He is the One who will sustain it. We also need to remember that we are nothing without God. Acts 17:28 puts this in perspective when it says, "For in Him we live and move and have our being. As some of your own poets have said, we are His offspring" (NIV). This solidifies the fact that we can do nothing worthwhile without God. Even those who do not serve God are still only being kept because of His grace. This scripture emphasizes that humility is the key to God's best.

> All of you, clothe yourselves with humility toward one another, because God opposes the proud but shows favor to the humble. Humble yourselves, therefore, under God's mighty hand, that He may lift you up in due time. (1 Peter 5:5b-6 NIV)

If we want to experience the favor of God, we must remain humble.

Quiet strength

God has provided us with quiet strength or gentleness. We don't have to be rough or abrasive but we can choose to be calm and watch God work things out for us, showing us which direction to take when we arrive at a crossroad. Instead of being strong in our own might, we can be strong in the Lord and in the power of *His* might (Ephesians 6:10). He always knows the right thing to do.

Sometimes, we get so worked up about things and we lash out in frustration, but God nudges us gently saying "Chill out. It's already been taken care of." I had such an experience, when at the beginning of the school year, my son needed some exercise books from the school. I went to purchase the books and was told that they had run out of certain colors. Now each subject was color-coded and he really needed a specific colored book to complete an assignment. So I started to get frustrated. I asked the bookstore clerk how they could be out of the books on the third day of school. She said they had to order more of them. All I was thinking was, "How is my child going to complete this assignment without the required book?" I allowed this to ruin the rest of the afternoon, fussing my children out for the least little thing, instead of leaving it to God and allowing that quiet strength to prevail. The next day, I asked my husband to take our son to the bookstore to get whatever other notebooks were available and inquire about the out of stock book again. He called me to let me know they had restocked and our son was able to get all of the notebooks he needed, including the one that was unavailable the day before. I sat back and marveled at how good God is and He said to me, "Now look how much time you wasted, thinking about something I already had covered. Rest in Me. Be strong in Me." It was a powerful lesson that I have determined I am going to apply to all other areas of my life.

Patience

In addition, instead of doing what we feel like doing when we feel like doing it, exercise discipline. It is the world's way to get what it wants when it wants it. Everyone seems to be in a rush to have it all. God made us and knows how much we can handle of anything… good or bad. So, He has designed a process for us to go through to get to where He would have us to be. If we run ahead of His plan, we will not be ready to handle the pressures of the next level. We must be patient and wait on Him as He teaches us certain lessons so that we are equipped and dressed in the clothing needed for the next part of the journey. I am reminded of God's promise to Israel:

> I will send my terror ahead of you and throw into confusion every nation you encounter. I will make all your enemies turn their backs and run. I will send the hornet ahead of you to drive the Hivites, Canaanites and Hittites out of your way. But I will not drive them out in a single year, because the land would become desolate and the wild animals too numerous for you. Little by little I will drive them out before you, until you have increased enough to take possession of the land. (Exodus 23:27-30 NIV)

God had prepared a place for His people, the children of Israel. He promised to drive out and get rid of all the enemies and roadblocks in their way. However, He explained that it would not have been beneficial to them if He destroyed their enemies too quickly and allowed them access into the land right away. This is because they would have been unable to maintain the land and there would be too many animals left there to threaten their vitality and sustainability. Therefore, God's plan for them was to deal with their enemies in small doses until the Israelites had grown enough to handle the entire parcel of land. Now suppose they had complained and demanded that God give them all that He had for them at one time. What would have been the result? First of all, they would not have been able to manage the resources and would have probably been destroyed by the ferocious beasts that they had not grown big enough to handle.

Isn't it the same with us? Yes we know that God has great plans in store for us, but we want everything instantly and are not prepared to wait on God's perfect timing. If we get it all at one time, God knows that it may be too much for us to handle, because we are not at that spiritual maturity level yet. Also, there may be some beasts on that path that we do not have the courage to face as yet. So, our Heavenly Father's word to us is "to be patient. I am working and allowing you to build yourselves up in the most holy faith, day by day, so that when you reach this course of the race, you will be able to embrace it with tenacity and courage and will not turn back, give in or drop out, but you will press through." So, let us determine to clothe ourselves with patience.

Even-temperdness

The next piece of spiritual clothing we need to put on if we are going to be spiritually fit to go the distance is even-temperedness. This means that we are balanced in our emotions and do not become easily angered, upset or frustrated when things do not go according to our plan. Remember that God has promised us...

> 'For I know the plans I have for you,' declares the Lord, 'plans to prosper you and not to harm you, plans to give you a hope and a future.' (Jeremiah 29:11 NIV)

The Google definition of temper is "a person's state of mind seen in terms of their being angry or calm." So being even tempered means deciding to be calm even when things are difficult. We make up our minds that no matter what happens, we will not become alarmed, fly off the handle or be moved to wrath, but rather we will approach each situation the way God would and choose peace and an assurance that God is in control. Why? Well because the above scripture assures us that God has a good plan for our lives. So, even though everything we face may not be good, God has a unique way of working all things out for our good, because we love Him (Romans 8:28). Therefore, we can choose not to become ruffled or uneasy.

Be the best "you"

Next, God encourages us to be content with second place. In this world where competition is so prevalent, this piece of garment may be challenging for many of us. The world tells us that first place is so important and so we strive to be first.

My sons have been involved in track and field for many years and all they think about sometimes is how they want to come in first and beat everyone. They have their electronic games and are constantly racing against each other trying to reach the finish line first. Even we as adults have gifts and talents and we get bent out of shape if someone can do what we do better than us, or if someone appears to be more successful than us. On our jobs, we are in a race to get to the top, because that is what society says success is and if we can just be first, we may feel better about ourselves. We get our worth from a standard that is less than God's standard. Can I tell you that there are many lonely people at the top? The root of having to be at the top is pride. We want to feel superior to others and be the best at everything. However, God is saying just be the best 'you' you can be. If everyone does likewise then this world would be transformed for Him, because we will all be doing our part.

> So since we find ourselves fashioned into all of these excellently formed and marvelously functioning parts in Christ's body, let's just go ahead and be what we were meant to be, without enviously or pridefully comparing ourselves with each other, or trying to be something we aren't. (Romans 12:6 MSG)

God created us to bring Him glory – to please Him, not to please people. Determine to be YOU – nobody else but YOU – and second place will be a non-issue.

Forgiveness that leads to kindness

We must also be clothed in forgiveness. If we are to run an effective and victorious race, we have to be quick to forgive. If we don't forgive quickly then we take on unnecessary baggage that will slow us down or cause us to come to a complete stop. Unforgiveness eats away at our core and makes us spiritually sick. Eventually we will become too weak to run our race. Romans 12:14 admonishes us to "bless those who persecute us; bless and do not curse." In subsequent verses, we are given clear instructions on how to deal with offense.

Do not repay anyone evil for evil. Be careful to do what is right in the eyes of everyone. If it is possible, as far as it depends on you, live at peace with everyone. Do not take revenge, my dear friends, but leave room for God's wrath, for it is written: 'It is Mine to avenge, I will repay,' says the Lord. On the contrary, 'if your enemy is hungry, feed him; if he is thirsty, give him something to drink. In doing this, you will heap burning coals on his head. Do not be overcome by evil, but overcome evil with good.' (Romans 12:17-20 NIV)

God says the way to respond to an offense is not unforgiveness but rather kindness. When we are kind to those who do us wrong, they are surprised because the world's way is to retaliate. Our kind actions cause them to pause and consider what they have done and they may even become repentant and consider a change of their course. This is what Jesus did for us. The Bible says, "While we were yet sinners, Christ died for us." He did not wait until we got ourselves together or got everything all figured out, felt repentant or sorry, or knew how to run this race. Before we could work out any of these details, Christ was willing and did die to secure our redemption. Hallelujah! Even while on the cross, when people hurled insults at Him and treated Him unkindly, He begged the Father "forgive them for they know not what they do" (Luke 23:34). He responded with kindness and mercy and that is what we are to do as we follow Him.

Love

Then finally, God has made available to us the best piece of apparel that money can't buy: LOVE. He said that out of all of these, make sure we have on our love suit in this race as it is appropriate for any weather we face. I believe that God's love makes all of the other pieces of the garment functional and operational. If we try to put on the other pieces and leave out love, we will not have much success. 1 Corinthians 13 makes this clear.

If I speak in the tongues of men or of angels, but do not have love, I am only a resounding gong or a clanging cymbal. If I have the gift of

> prophecy and can fathom all mysteries and all knowledge, and if I have
> a faith that can move mountains, but do not have love, I am nothing.
> If I give all I possess to the poor and give over my body to hardship that
> I may boast, but do not have love, I gain nothing.
>
> (1 Corinthians 13:1-3 NIV)

So, it is safe to say that no matter what good we try to do in our own strength, without the love of God in our hearts motivating our actions, it will amount to nothing in His eyes. This should be a sobering thought for us and cause us to check our motives constantly. Is it a good thing or a God thing?

> Love is patient, love is kind. It does not envy, it does not boast, it is not
> proud. It does not dishonor others, it is not self-seeking, it is not easily
> angered, it keeps no record of wrongs. Love does not delight in evil
> but rejoices in the truth. It always protects, always trust, always hopes,
> always perseveres. (1 Corinthians 13:4-7 NIV)

We can really see in these verses that all of the other pieces of the garment we discussed above are dependent upon the love of God being present and prevalent in our hearts. God's love in us will motivate us to be different and act differently. This is what changes the people around us and impacts this world for God.

Reject spiritual junk

Now that we understand what the proper attire is for our big race, we need to turn our attention to our spiritual intake? We must realize that spiritually we cannot eat whatever we like without giving thought to the impact it would have on our spiritual lives. We have to be cognizant of what we allow ourselves to absorb. If we feed on the spiritual garbage that is so prevalent in our world today broadcasted on our televisions, radios, social media etc., then we are bound to become spiritually lethargic and will not be able to run effectively. However, when we feed on the right things, we will get the spiritual nourishment we need to endure whatever comes our way during this race we call life. What are we feeding on spiritually so that we will have the power to endure in this marathon?

The right stuff

If we intend to finish the race and finish strong, then we must make the Word of God our daily spiritual food. Psalm 1 expounds on the importance of the Word of God in our lives. Verses 1-3 tell us the kind of person who is blessed and empowered to prosper during this race of life.

> Happy are those who reject the advice of evil people, who do not follow the example of sinners or join those who have no use for God. Instead, they find joy in obeying the Law of the Lord, and they study it day and night. They are like trees that grow beside a stream, that bear fruit at the right time, and whose leaves do not dry up. They succeed in everything they do. (Psalm 1:1-3 GNT)

When we meditate on God's Word, God promises that we will have a continual supply of His living water to sustain us, daily. We are compared to well-watered and nourished trees that produce good fruit at the right time. We are never dry or withered in our faith because we are continually feeding on the Word of God that is able to save our souls. As a result, we are successful at whatever we make up our minds to do. Why? It is because we are led by the Word of God. When we focus on God and His Word, we will have the road map that will enable us to reach our destination. There may be times of darkness along the path, but the Word of God will be God's light to lead us in the direction that leads to life and peace. It doesn't matter how rough the terrain, or how steep the hill, God's Word will give us the spiritual fortitude and strength to push through the difficulties and setbacks and press on in the process.

Being led by God's Holy Spirit will also make us spiritually fit to go the distance. When we receive Jesus Christ as our Savior and Lord, the Holy Spirit, Who is the third part of the Trinity (God the Father, God the Son and God the Holy Spirit) comes to live in us along with the Father and the Son. Jesus said that the Holy Spirit is a revealer and our teacher. John 14:17 says, "He is the Spirit who reveals the truth about God." John 14:26 also says, "The Helper, The Holy Spirit, whom the

Father will send in My Name, will teach you everything and make you remember all that I have told you." So it is critical that we not only have the Holy Spirit dwelling in us, but we must allow Him to reveal God's truth to us and remind us what God expects of us as His children.

In essence, we must be led by the Spirit of God with every step we take. He cannot remain dormant in our lives, if we expect to run an effective race for God. He provides the living water our souls thirst for by filling us with the very presence of God. He dissects the Word of God so that we can understand it more clearly and become doers of the Word as instructed in James:

> Don't fool yourself into thinking that you are a listener when you are anything but, letting the Word go in one ear and out the other. Act on what you hear! Those who hear and don't act are like those who glance in the mirror, walk away, and two minutes later have no idea who they are, what they look like. But whoever catches a glimpse of the revealed counsel of God – the free life! – even out of the corner of his eye, and sticks with it, is no distracted scatterbrain but a man or woman of action. That person will find delight and affirmation in the action.
>
> (James 1:23-25 MSG)

God's intention is not just for us to read His Word but also meditate on it so that we will gain His understanding of how we are to live for Him. If we look at it without really taking it in, then the Word will not have a chance to take root in our hearts so that we will have the ability to endure during the rough patches of life. James says if we stick with the Word, then and only then we will find delight (pleasure, the good life) in the actions we take. Why? I believe it is because we are being governed by the Word of God!

The last part of the spiritual fitness required for us to endure to the end is the application of the whole armor of God, which was expounded upon in detail in an earlier chapter.

Remember, God has already provided the spiritual clothing we need to be successful in our life for Him. All we have to do is SUIT UP!

CHAPTER 7

THE MIND OF CHRIST

We have just learned about the spiritual clothing God has made available for us to run an effective and victorious race for Him. Looking at my own race, I have discovered that if we are to accomplish our goals by fulfilling God's purpose for our lives, we have to look to our perfect example: Jesus Christ. He came to earth and ran a perfect race. How did He do this? I believe it was all in the way He thought and the way He looked at things through Spirit eyes. He saw things from God's perspective. He had the purpose of His Father God always before Him, always on His mind. If we hope to be successful, we need to think like Jesus did, so we can act like Jesus did and finish like Jesus did: VICTORIOUS! WE NEED THE MIND OF CHRIST!

As we look through the scriptures, we see several things that portray the thought process of Jesus.

He was always about His Father's business

When we first encounter the young Jesus in the scriptures, he is twelve years old. Luke's gospel (2:41-52) records a temple visit by Jesus and his family. It tells us that every year, Jesus' parents went to Jerusalem for the Passover feast. When he was twelve, he accompanied them on this trip. After the feast was over, Jesus' parents began the journey home and assumed that Jesus was in their caravan even though they did not see Him. Of course, where else would a normal twelve-year old boy be? After church, He should have been more than ready to return home. However, after an entire day of travel, they were unable to locate Him among their relatives. What could possibly be going through their minds at this time? I am sure they were anxious and afraid, as any concerned parent would be. Verse 48 confirms this. Had He been kidnapped? Did He wonder off with friends? Had He gotten Himself into trouble? They returned to Jerusalem and had to search for Him for another three days before they found Him... Where? IN THE TEMPLE! It was probably the last place they looked. They had probably searched for Him at all of the kid-friendly and fun spots, first. What twelve-year old boy would want to spend extra time in the temple (in God's presence), wanting to know more about God? I'm sure it just seemed peculiar to them!

However, that is exactly where they found Him.

> Three days later they found Him in the [court of the] temple, sitting among the teachers, both listening to them and asking them questions. All who heard Him were amazed by His intelligence and His understanding and His answers. (Luke 2:46-47 AMP)

It is evident that Jesus was different from the average boy His age. But what made Him different? It was His passion for the things of God. Age becomes irrelevant when God's passion takes hold of you. When Mary, His mother, confronted Him, this was His reply: "How is it that you had to look for Me? Did you not see and know that it is necessary (as a duty) for Me to be in My Father's house and (occupied) about My Father's business?" What a profound statement of commitment from a young boy. He recognized that it was not only necessary, but a requirement for Him to be concerned about the things His Father (God) was concerned about. That was His focus and I believe that was why He was able to run the splendid race He did, and leave an extraordinary example for us to follow.

Some of us may not be twelve years old, but we indeed have a race to run for our Great King. Do we crave the presence of God in our daily lives and activities? Are we passionate about the things of God? Many times we allow things, people and situations to crowd out the voice of God and the plans He has for our lives. It is only when we make God our first priority that we begin to experience the true victory that is ours in Christ Jesus.

So wherever we are in our course right now, we need to remember that the key to our victory is to be "about our Father's business", like Jesus was. He had an earthly Father and so do we, but we are to ensure that we are tapped into the heart of our spiritual Father, God. When we set our allegiance to His plan for our lives, we will possess the mental stamina and fortitude to "press on toward the goal to win the (supreme and heavenly) prize to which God in Christ Jesus is calling us upward (Phil. 3:14)."

Jesus was willing to surrender it all

In Heaven, Jesus had everything. He had it made. Nothing was lacking. After all, He was equal to God the Father Himself. However, when humankind had a need, Jesus was ready and willing to surrender it all for the sake of our fallen state.

> Let this mind be in you, which was also in Christ Jesus.
> (Philippians 2:5 NKJV)

What is this mind that Paul is talking about? He goes on to explain the mind of Christ in the verses that follow.

> He had equal status with God but didn't think so much of Himself that He had to cling to the advantages of that status no matter what. Not at all. When the time came, He set aside the privileges of deity and took on the status of a slave, became human! Having become human, he stayed human. It was an incredibly humbling process. He didn't claim special privileges. Instead, He lived a selfless, obedient life and then died a selfless, obedient death – and the worst kind of death at that – a crucifixion. (Philippians 2:6-8 MSG)

This was the most unselfish act ever committed in the history of mankind. God Himself, in the person of Jesus Christ, surrendered all of His privileges in Heaven, to save a lost and dying world. What would motivate our Savior to do such a thing? The answer is unselfish love. Jesus loved us more than the pleasures of Heaven. He saw our brokenness and was moved to restore us to our rightful place as kings and queens on the earth. Suppose Jesus had said, "Well I have got it made, so too bad for them?" Where would we be? However, that was not His nature or His mindset. He had a mindset that was sacrificial in nature. He gave up everything, so that we could have access to everything God wanted us to have.

AMAZING LOVE, the songwriter says, rings so true when we think of all He sacrificed for us. He didn't just sacrifice His deity, but also His physical comforts and more importantly, His very own body, which He allowed to be crucified to secure our redemption. WHAT A SAVIOR!

Yet, today, we find it so hard to sacrifice an hour in prayer, or to give of ourselves for the sake of the betterment of others in need. Their needs may not be only physical, but also emotional, spiritual, financial, mental and relational. Many times we have an "all for me" attitude. As long as we have what we need, we're fine, and we don't take the time to think about others around us. And even if we do, we will help as long as it doesn't take us out of our comfort zone.

If we intend to run a successful race, we have to stop living isolated lives, cut off from and blinded to the needs of those around us at work, at church, in the food store, in our own families or neighborhoods. We must be willing to sacrifice our time, talents and treasure for them, to help make their lives the most fulfilling lives they can have by God's grace. It shouldn't be enough that we have all we need, but we should have the mindset of Christ that makes us want to ensure that everyone has an opportunity to have their best life ever. That is why Jesus left His place in Heaven, so that we could also have a place in Heaven with Him.

We know that we are running an efficient race, when we care about where other people are at and want to ensure that they have access to what we have and they are running their best race as well. Jesus was willing to be humbled, so that we could be exalted. This is a key component to having the mind of Christ.

Jesus did not have to remain in His humbled state however, because after He had completed His work of salvation, the Bible tells us that God highly exalted Him.

> Because of that obedience, God lifted Him high and honored Him far beyond anyone or anything, ever, so that all created beings in heaven and on earth – even those long ago dead and buried – will bow in worship before this Jesus Christ, and call out in praise that He is the Master of all, to the glorious honor of God the Father.
>
> (Philippians 2:9-11 MSG)

What a reward! God honored Jesus' willingness to surrender it all and promoted Him. I believe that if we are willing to sacrifice everything for God, He will honor us and promote us as well. That should not be the motivation for doing what we do, but it is simply one of the benefits of living an obedient and surrendered life.

Jesus was focused on His work

Jesus had 33 years to complete His Work. If we knew the amount of time we have been given to finish our work for our Father, many of us may begin to panic, because time may be running out. However, if we, like Jesus, determine early on in life to surrender to God and begin to live out His purpose for our lives, then we will have no need to fear if we will finish our course or not. God has given every one of us the opportunity to begin and finish our work for Him. It is up to us whether or not we will embrace this opportunity. Be assured that we also have enough time to complete our purpose, but it all depends on if we will stay focused and remain on task, or if we will become easily distracted and get off course because of worldly enticements or even troubles. If we follow Jesus' example of staying focused on the assignment, we will be more than conquerors in our race.

After being baptized by His cousin John, receiving God's seal of approval and successfully resisting the temptations of the devil, Jesus returned from the wilderness and immediately began His public ministry. With undaunted focus, He began to proclaim the coming of the Kingdom of God on the earth. He was intimately acquainted with His mission, which He read while in the synagogue in His hometown of Nazareth. This is documented in the following verses.

> God's Spirit is on Me; He's chosen Me to preach the Message of good news to the poor, sent Me to announce pardon to prisoners and recovery of sight to the blind, to set the burdened and battered free, to announce, 'This is God's year to act! (Luke 4:18-19 MSG)

Immediately after Jesus confirmed that this was His purpose, He began His healing, deliverance and teaching ministry. In this very same chapter of Luke, He healed a man who was possessed by demons by driving them out of him. He also commanded a fever to leave the mother-in-law of Simon Peter, his disciple, and she arose immediately freed from the fever and began to cook dinner for Him.

For thirty years, Jesus stood in obscurity quietly preparing for His public ministry. When the time was right, He stepped out of the shadows and powerfully revolutionized the way people thought and lived with His message of salvation and freedom. People did not have to live in bondage to sin, sickness, lack, demonic oppression or possession any longer because the Kingdom of God had come to earth through Jesus Christ.

He had three years to complete His public ministry and this purpose was the driving force of His life. It determined where He went, who He touched, who He surrounded Himself with and how He spent His time. If you study the Gospels you will see that not one minute was wasted. In verses 42-44 of the same chapter, Jesus said to the crowd who clung to Him so He couldn't go on, "Don't you realize that there are yet other villages where I have to tell the Message of God's kingdom, that this is the work God has sent me to do?" He knew He had to stay focused and remain on task if He was to be successful in completing His race.

We need to take our cue from Jesus' life and determine to stay on task. First, we have to find out what God has called us to do. Then we need to spend time in His presence, preparing for the work that we must do, so that when God is ready to release us to our mission field, we would have the mental stamina to press through no matter what the resistance. Kindly note that our mission field does not necessarily mean a foreign country, full time ministry or preaching in front of thousands. It could be the classroom where you teach, the department where you work, your neighborhood association group, the customers in the store where you work, a prison ministry or an afterschool class or club.

Wherever it is, God wants you to be equipped to change lives. This happens only if we spend time with Him in prayer, reading His Word and basking in His presence to receive His instructions. If you haven't begun doing this as yet, start by spending five minutes praying and reading each day. Give God an opportunity to speak to you for five minutes. You will be surprised at what He has to say. He will begin to tell you where He wants you to go and what He wants you to say and do. This will help you to stay on task and steady in your daily race of life. Even if others try to distract or detain you like the crowds tried to do to Jesus in the above verse, you will know what your goal is, stay focused and have God's supernatural enabling power to press through and complete it.

Jesus was focused on the needs of others

The focus of Jesus' ministry was on serving others. He taught His disciples this valuable lesson when just before He was crucified, He got a bowl and began to wash their feet. This was a symbol of servanthood.

Some did not want Him to "stoop to this level" and thought that if anyone's feet deserved to be washed, it was Jesus'. However, in the Kingdom of God, we are called to serve, not to be served as Jesus illustrated this through this act.

Jesus spent His entire ministry focusing on the needs of others. He came to earth and showed us the way we should live our lives in service to God by serving others. He was constantly interrupted by persons who desperately required His assistance. He raised Jairus' daughter from the dead, and even on the way to her house took the time to restore wholeness to a woman who had suffered from an issue of blood for twelve years. He raised a widow's son from the dead in the middle of the funeral procession. He healed the centurion's servant and the Syrophoenician woman's daughter who didn't, at that time, even have legal access to His power.

Compassion is what drove Jesus to do what He did. He was concerned about those who were suffering. He had the power to give them a better life and He exercised that power on their behalf. Jesus not only recognized their needs but was also moved to do what He could to meet those needs.

One story in particular showed the compassion of Jesus in action and exemplified how important it was to Him to focus on others rather than self. This story is the feeding of the five thousand people as recorded in all four of the gospels. Here is Mark's gospel's account:

> The apostles then rendezvoused with Jesus and reported on all that they had done and taught. Jesus said, 'Come off by yourselves; let's take a break and get a little rest.' For there was constant coming and going. They didn't even have time to eat. So they got in the boat and went off to a remote place by themselves. Someone saw them going and the word got around. From the surrounding towns people went out on foot, running, and got there ahead of them. When Jesus arrived, he saw this huge crowd. At the sight of them, his heart broke—like sheep with no shepherd they were. He went right to work teaching them. When his disciples thought this had gone on long enough—it was now quite late in the day—they interrupted: 'We are a long way out in

the country, and it's very late. Pronounce a benediction and send these folks off so they can get some supper.' Jesus said, 'You do it. Fix supper for them.' They replied, 'Are you serious? You want us to go spend a fortune on food for their supper?' But he was quite serious. 'How many loaves of bread do you have? Take an inventory.' That didn't take long. 'Five,' they said, 'plus two fish.' Jesus got them all to sit down in groups of fifty or a hundred—they looked like a patchwork quilt of wildflowers spread out on the green grass! He took the five loaves and two fish, lifted His face to heaven in prayer, blessed, broke, and gave the bread to the disciples, and the disciples in turn gave it to the people. He did the same with the fish. They all ate their fill. The disciples gathered twelve baskets of leftovers. More than five thousand were at the supper.

(Mark 6:30-44 MSG)

When Jesus saw the desperation of the crowds who ran seeking after Him, the passage said His heart broke. In other words, He was filled with so much compassion that He felt compelled to do something to deliver them from brokenness, point them in the right direction, and place them on the path of life and peace. These people had followed Jesus and forsaken human needs such as eating, drinking or resting, just so they could hear the words of healing and restoration from their Messiah. When Jesus decided to feed them supper, it demonstrated that He was not only concerned about their spiritual and emotional state, but their physical well-being as well. He was concerned about every aspect of their lives.

The disciples saw with natural eyes that the crowd was hungry but automatically concluded that it was physically impossible to feed this large group of people, even though they had seen the miracle working power of Jesus in action before. Their solution was simple: send them away to buy their own food. However, Jesus challenged them by asking them to provide dinner for these people. What was their response? "Are You serious", or in essence, "Have You lost it? We are incapable of doing what You asked." They focused on their inabilities, but Jesus was focused on the needs of the crowd who were harassed, bothered and had sacrificed so much just to be with Him and hear His teaching.

Yes, it would have certainly been easier to send the crowds away. That is generally our way of doing things – to pass the buck or put the responsibility on someone else. This is rooted in selfishness. On the other hand, God's way is to go the extra mile by going out of the way to help someone in need!

This is a lesson for us because if we are to run a fulfilling race, we have to sometimes forsake our own needs, comforts, rights and privileges and turn our attention to the other runners around us who are at that time harassed, bothered, hungry and discouraged. God is calling us to reach out our hands to lift these people up so that they can begin to run again. When we begin to help them, God will multiply our efforts, meet their needs with what we offer Him in such a magnificent way that there will be more than enough for everyone, as the crowd in this story experienced! From two small fish and five loaves of bread, five thousand men – not counting the women and children – were fed and twelve baskets of food were left over. This all happened because Jesus encouraged His disciples to see and focus on the needs of others.

Where is our focus? Are we focusing on our own needs or are we looking with Spirit eyes to see the persons who God places on our paths, so that we can be a blessing to them and be His hands and feet on this earth? That is how we run a race that is both noteworthy and peculiar, one that people will take notice of as different from the norm, thereby bringing honor and glory to God!

Miracles are waiting to occur, but God is waiting for us to see the opportunities He is placing before us. Step out in faith and watch Him do something supernatural in the life of someone who needs His grace! We are the hands and feet of God on this earth.

Jesus knew where to turn when things got difficult

It is interesting that immediately after Jesus had performed this great miracle, His next step was to send His disciples ahead to the other side of the lake, so that He could commune with His Father and refuel for the mission. He recognized the importance of reconnecting and being rejuvenated by the Source (the Real Power Source), God Himself.

> As soon as the meal was finished, He insisted that the disciples get in the boat and go on ahead to the other side while He dismissed the people. With the crowd dispersed, He climbed the mountain so He could be by Himself and pray. He stayed there alone, late into the night.
>
> (Matthew 14:22-23 MSG)

He had just expended a lot of energy, taught and fed five thousand people. After pouring out of Himself, He exercised wisdom by taking the time to reconnect, refuel and be refreshed in the presence of God. After spending this time, Jesus rejoined the disciples and another miracle occurred, He walked on water to meet them in the boat. On the other side, people were waiting to experience His ministry of healing and restoration. Therefore, Jesus was constantly stopping at the Heavenly gas station to refuel. So many of us expect miracles, but we never take time to commune with the Miracle Worker. We want all of the sparks without the Divine connection. Jesus' mental decision here to constantly go back to the Source is a key ingredient to a life of breakthrough, victory and miracles.

We constantly see Jesus taking these "station identifications".

> Now it came to pass in those days that He went out to the mountain to pray, and continued all night in prayer to God. (Luke 6:12 NIV)

The next day, Jesus selected the twelve apostles. This was a big decision because these were the men to whom He would entrust His ministry of reconciliation after He was gone. Therefore, a huge decision like this required an all-night prayer vigil, where He received specific instructions from God. When we turn to God for refueling, He not only recharges us for the next mission, but He also gives us Divine directions and the wisdom to make the best choices in life. This is something we desperately need if we desire to run a successful race. We must stay connected to our Power Source, so that we have the spiritual stamina to finish our course.

Before Jesus began His ministry after His baptism, He withdrew to the wilderness for a time of prayer and fasting that lasted forty days. There, He was tempted by the devil, but because He had been in the Presence of God, He was well equipped with God's Word and power to overthrow the devil's plans to bring Him down. With each temptation, Jesus returned with the overcoming words, "It is written". Then when He had successfully resisted the temptations, we are told, "Angels came and ministered to Him."

Mark 1 again shows Jesus retreating into the presence of God.

> While it was still night, way before dawn, he got up and went out to a secluded spot and prayed. Simon and those with him went looking for him. They found him and said, 'Everybody's looking for you.'
>
> (Mark 1:35 MSG)

Yes, everyone may have been looking for Him, but He knew that He must be about His Father's business to get the instructions and the power to do the work. Before dawn, He was up seeking the Father's face to know what direction to take. Then He was prepared when the disciples found Him saying that people needed Him.

Jesus did not get entangled with the fame or the demands on His life for ministry, but rather He got entangled with the Father so that He could meet the needs of the people in a manageable way. He did not become overwhelmed with their press into Him, but always connected with God Who gave Him the strength and wisdom to accomplish His mission. We must choose to do likewise.

There will always be a demand on us to do more than we can do in these finite bodies. Therefore, we need to stay in constant communion with God for wisdom, direction, strength and power to do what He has called us to do. That is the only way we will possess endurance for the journey. Jesus knew how to put first things first. We need to emulate His example!

Therefore, when Jesus came to the "fork in the road" in His life, His final hours and things became really difficult, Jesus was completely prepared, because He had spent a lifetime of putting this principle into practice. What did He do on the night that He was betrayed into the hands of sinful men? He withdrew and retreated into His Father's loving arms and comforting Presence for the final time in His earth suit.

> He pulled away from them about a stone's throw, knelt down, and prayed, 'Father, remove this cup from me. But please, not what I want. What do you want?' At once an angel from heaven was at his side, strengthening him. He prayed on all the harder. Sweat, wrung from him like drops of blood, poured off his face. (Luke 22:41-44 MSG)

While in the Garden of Gethsemane, in the final hours of His life, Jesus was torn between His flesh wanting to live, asking God to let the cup of suffering pass from Him, and His spirit knowing that it was time to fulfill God's salvation plan for mankind. Jesus knew where to turn and Who to turn to in this time, because He had done it so many times before. He turned to His Father and poured His heart out to Him about how difficult the path was that He was about to take. It was there in God's presence that He found the strength, power and peace needed to secure our redemption, even though His flesh fought against Him to give up on the mission and throw in the towel.

How many times do we find ourselves in a difficult situation, when we know what God wants, but we are bombarded by our flesh that wants to abandon the cause of Christ? We allow our fears, worries and apprehensions to take over. Jesus, our Great High Priest has already been there and has shown us that we must turn to God in those times of physical, emotional, mental and spiritual weakness to receive supernatural strength from the Heavenly throne room.

If you are at that place of breaking right now in your race, I invite you to withdraw to a quiet place into the arms of your loving, Heavenly Father and find the rest, reassurance and recharging you need to continue to run your race and fulfill God's purpose for your life!

Jesus understood the importance of leaving a legacy

When Jesus came to earth, He came with the purpose of being the Savior of the world. His time here was short, 33 years as I mentioned earlier. He had 3 years of public ministry to share with the people of that time and generation about the Kingdom of Heaven. However, God's plan was for this message to continue throughout the ages of time so that even today we could be partakers of God's limitless grace. Therefore, in order for the saving work of God to continue after His death, resurrection and ascension, Jesus would have to impart His life, spirit and ministry into others who would be given the mantle of continuing His work here on earth. He had to leave a legacy for others to follow!

After He returned from being tempted in the wilderness by the devil for 40 days and nights, we find Jesus walking along the Sea of Galilee. It is here at the outset of His ministry that He began to select those men in whom He would reproduce Himself. Jesus calls His first disciples:

> As Jesus was walking beside the Sea of Galilee, He saw two brothers, Simon called Peter and his brother Andrew. They were casting a net into the lake, for they were fishermen. 'Come, follow me,' Jesus said, 'and I will send you out to fish for people.' At once they left their nets and followed Him. Going on from there, He saw two brothers, James son of Zebedee and his brother John. They were in the boat with their father Zebedee, preparing their nets. Jesus called them, and immediately they left the boat and their father and followed Him.
>
> (Matthew 4:18-22 NIV)

From the outset of His ministry, Jesus selected His successors. As He went along, Jesus chose eight other men to join these first four. He knew His physical mission here would be short, but that the work He started had to be passed on to others so it could be continued. Therefore, before any miracle was performed or any teaching taught, He chose men who would hear what He said and witness what He did, so they could continue to teach others about His great life and perform miracles in His mighty name. It is interesting that when called to follow Jesus, there was no hesitation, but they left behind everything: their jobs, livelihood and families to follow the divine call on their lives. They did not know Jesus. All they knew was fishing, but it was something about His call that spoke to their very spirits and they knew that they should follow this man even though they may not have known where or why.

If only we could be so willing to abandon our way of doing and being to follow the divine call of God on our lives. It may not be about leaving our jobs and families, but it may simply be the call to say, "Yes Jesus, I want You to be in control of my life. I want to be used for Your purposes, so that someone may know through my life that You came to save them." Many times, we refuse to follow if we don't have all of the answers, all the pieces to the puzzle, when God is saying to us, "Just come. I have all the answers. Just follow My lead." The first disciples didn't ask where, why, how or who. They simply followed! And they became the ones who carried on the legacy of Jesus Christ.

Jesus came for the world but He spent most of His three years of public ministry teaching these men the ways of the Kingdom of God. In Matthew's gospel, in particular, for three chapters Jesus taught the Sermon on the Mount.

> Now when Jesus saw the crowds, he went up on a mountainside and sat down. His disciples came to him, and he began to teach them.
> (Matthew 5:1-2 NIV)

Yes the crowds may have been benefactors of this teaching, but this verse expressly states that Jesus went into teaching mode with His disciples. He taught them the Beatitudes (the Blessings of God: Matthew 5:4-11). He taught them that they were to be the salt and light of the world (Matthew 5:13-15). He also taught Kingdom principles on the law, adultery, divorce, making oaths, revenge and loving their enemies (Matthew 5:17-48). He showed them the power of giving, praying and fasting (Matthew 6:1-18). He explained the importance of securing treasures in Heaven rather than on earth as well as why they should not become anxious or worried (Matthew 6:19-34). They were also instructed not to judge others, to ask and depend on God for what they needed, to enter the Kingdom of God by the narrow gate, how to discern the difference between true and false prophets, what God expects of a true disciple and what makes one a wise builder (Matthew 7:1-29).

The disciples, and by extension the crowds, got an earful during that sermon. Jesus taught life principles that were essential for them to fulfill the call and complete their mission. The disciple Matthew obviously placed incredible value on the lessons being learned and took a lot of notes, because He gave the most detailed account of this life-changing message. As a result, we, the modern day disciples are benefitting from what Matthew documented, because we depend on these verses so much as we seek to live the lives to which God has called us. Matthew listened, recorded and passed on the keys to the life-giving Kingdom of God. He received the message, passed it on to others, and the legacy of Jesus' work continued. That is why Jesus spent so much time and energy with His disciples so that He could get what He had inside of Him birthed in them. They, in turn, passed it down to the generations after them and the message endured. That is what a person who knows the importance of succession planning and legacy will do.

The legacy has now been passed on to you and me and it is our turn to ensure that the message of the Kingdom of God endures to the future generations that will come after us. It is our time to hear from God and declare it to the next generation. There may be principles that God is whispering to you right now based on His Word and proven way of doing things in the world. God is depending on you to listen, document and pass on to others who may come after you so that the gospel of Jesus may continue to be preached to the ends of the earth.

This should give us an injection of faith, focus and strength as we run our race. We do not run without purpose or in vain. Our race is significant and our life important because we have the awesome task of passing on the message and, therefore, legacy of Jesus' life to those whom God has chosen to place in our paths.

Therefore, just from the life of Jesus, we see that our race is more mental than physical. We need to have a determined mindset to be successful in completing our course with distinction to make our God smile and say "Well done." We must recognize like Jesus did:

> The harvest is plentiful but the workers are few. Ask the Lord of the harvest, therefore, to send out workers into His harvest field.
>
> (Matthew 9:38)

Jesus understood the importance of His race and developed the mental stamina to complete His journey with excellence by always being about His Father's business, being willing to surrender it all, staying focused on His work, pausing to give attention to the needs of others, knowing Who to turn to when things got difficult and understanding the importance of leaving a legacy for others to follow.

This is a perfect example of how to run an excellent race, mentally, and come to a flourishing finish. We should determine today to employ these key elements and keep moving forward to the finish line!

CHAPTER 8

GUARD YOUR HEART

Now that we know how to mentally prepare ourselves for the journey ahead, there is another vital part that we must protect: the heart. Many times we face external obstacles, that is, the things that are done to us by others or inflicted on us by our spiritual enemy, the devil. We can't control when those attacks will come, but we have learned that "we are more than conquerors through Christ" (Romans 8:37). However, there are many internal battles we face during our race that can be just as detrimental to our success as the external attacks. So we must be careful of the kinds of things we allow to take root in our hearts.

Proverbs 4:23 NIV says, "Above all else, guard your heart, for everything you do flows from it." The King James Version says, "Keep thy heart with all diligence; for out of it are the issues of life." I like to merge the two by saying, "guard your heart for out of it flows the issues of life." Dictionary.com defines "issue" as "something that is sent out or put forward in any form" as well as "a point in question or a matter that is in dispute." So we can infer that what is in our hearts is what will flow out into our lives and relationships through our words and deeds. In addition, we can also assume that how we handle the matters or disputes in our lives demonstrates the condition of our hearts.

The center of life

The heart is the center of our body and distributes the blood to all of the other areas, bringing life to every cell and organ. In the same manner, our spiritual heart is the center of our spirit man, and pumps life throughout our spiritual body, bringing life to every part. If we allow our spiritual heart to be polluted and clogged with vices that destroy, then these "issues" will clog every area and threaten our spiritual vitality. I believe this is why King Solomon admonishes us to guard our hearts in the above verse.

What should we guard our hearts from? We have already discussed some of those things earlier, things such as fear. In chapter 6, we talked about things we should get rid of as Christians because these are ill-fitting clothes. I would like to highlight just a few of them.

Guard your heart from lust

Dictionary.com defines "lust" as an "uncontrolled or illicit sexual desire or appetite; a passionate or overwhelming desire or craving (usually followed by *for*)". Even though lust generally involves an uncontrolled sexual desire, it also refers to any uncontrolled desire or craving that is overpowering in our lives. God never intends for any desire in us to be out of control. The definition that God gave me is lust is "simply wanting what we should not have." The Bible encourages us to be self-controlled which is a fruit of the Holy Spirit that is borne in our lives when we submit to His will. Therefore, we must guard our hearts from lust, because it produces in us an unhealthy desire that is out of control.

> You know the next commandment pretty well, too: 'Don't go to bed with another's spouse.' But don't think you've preserved your virtue simply by staying out of bed. Your heart can be corrupted by lust even quicker than your body. Those leering looks you think nobody notices – they also corrupt. (Matthew 5:27-28 MSG)

When we allow our eyes to gaze on what we shouldn't then lust is birthed in our hearts. We see something or someone we know we shouldn't have, but we want it or them anyway. Even if we can't get what we want physically, we fantasize about what we have seen in our minds and are only waiting for the opportunity to act out what we have envisioned.

In the parable of the sower, Jesus explained to His disciples and by extension to us, the kinds of things that choke the Word of God and prevent it from being properly planted in our hearts and bearing fruit in our lives.

> And these are they [the seeds] which are sown among thorns; such as hear the Word. And the cares of this world, and the deceitfulness of riches, <u>and the lusts of other things entering in</u>, choke the Word, and it becometh unfruitful. (Mark 4:18-19)

When we allow lust to enter into our hearts, the Word of God is choked out of our lives and this threatens our spiritual vitality. Our heart has become corrupted or contaminated. What flows out of the heart, flows throughout the body, therefore our body also becomes contaminated.

So how do we guard our heart from lust? God's answer to lust is to exercise self-control as I mentioned above.

> But the fruit of the Spirit is love, joy, peace, forbearance, kindness, goodness, faithfulness, gentleness and <u>self-control</u>. Against such things there is no law. Those who belong to Christ Jesus have crucified the flesh with its passions and desires. Since we live by the Spirit, let us keep in step with the Spirit. Let us not become conceited, provoking and envying each other. (Galatians 5:22-26 NIV)

When we come into a relationship with God through Jesus Christ, His Son, we are given a new nature. Our new nature is not dominated by an overwhelming desire to get what we want even though it is wrong for us to have it. Our new nature can walk in self-discipline and temperance. We can say "No" to the wrong things and "Yes" to the God things. God's Spirit dwelling in us gives us the power to do just that. Galatians 5 also encourages us to "walk by the Spirit and you will not gratify the desires (lusts) of the flesh" (verse 16).

Today, let's make a determination to walk in God's ways and desire only what He wants us to have, confident of the fact that He created us and knows what's best for us. This may require refusing to look at (concentrate on) certain things or certain people. It will probably require a lot of prayer, meditation on the Word of God and in some cases, fasting.

Guard your heart from greed

Freedictionary.com defines greed as "an excessive desire to acquire or possess more than what one needs or deserves, especially with respect to material wealth".

> But godliness with contentment is great gain. For we brought nothing into the world and we can take nothing out of it. But if we have food and clothing, we will be content with that. Those who want to get rich fall into temptation and a trap and into many foolish and harmful desires that plunge people into ruin and destruction. For the love of money is the root of all kinds of evil. Some people, eager for money, have wandered from the faith and pierced themselves with many griefs.
> (1 Timothy 6:6-10 NIV)

These verses show us what can happen when our desire for money and wealth is out of control. Money in and of itself isn't bad. After all, King Solomon himself says, "Money answereth all things" (Ecclesiastes 10:19b). The problems come when we fall in love with it and will do anything and everything – such as lie, steal and cheat – just to have more of it.

When we do these things to obtain more money and wealth, this is an indication that money has become a god or idol in our lives. As we have learned from the verses in Mark 4, "the deceitfulness of riches" is another thing that chokes out the Word of God and makes it unfruitful.

I am not saying that God doesn't want us to have money. Of course, God wants us to prosper. He wants us to be able to pay our bills, have a roof over our heads, food to eat and clothes to wear. He also wants us to enjoy our lives, such as being able to afford a vacation or to celebrate a special occasion or accomplishment.

> Beloved, I wish above all things that thou mayest prosper and be in health, even as thy soul prospereth. (3 John 1:2)

As our souls prosper in the things of God, He promises prosperity and provision in our bodies and all the other aspects of our lives as well. This is because as we become more mature in Him, He knows He can begin to trust us with more of His resources. When we are good stewards of His blessings, then we receive more blessings from God. We can be trusted to use the money that flows to us not only to take care of our own needs, but also to help alleviate the burdens of others and also to advance God's kingdom. Therefore, those who recognize that God is their provider and the source of all blessings in their lives are less likely to hoard or grab at everything they can get. They know that their supply will never run out and whatever they need will be provided for them at the right time.

These are the people who have put money in its proper perspective and who do not succumb to greed. These are also the persons who will give a tithe (10%) of their gross income to God as instructed in Malachi:

> 'Bring the whole tithe into the storehouse, that there may be food in my house. Test me in this,' says the Lord Almighty, 'and see if I will not throw open the floodgates of heaven and pour out so much blessing that there will not be room enough to store it. I will prevent pests from devouring your crops, and the vines in your fields will not drop their fruit before it is ripe,' says the Lord Almighty. 'Then all the nations will call you blessed, for yours will be a delightful land,' says the Lord Almighty.' (Malachi 3:10-12 NIV)

When we give back to God what He asks of us, He promises a supernatural outpouring of His blessings in our lives that is simply too much for us to use for ourselves. Therefore, we are placed in a strategic position to bless others around us. The promise also includes protection from the enemy regarding our prosperity (it will not wither away) and success in all of our plans, as they will not be aborted. People will be able to see and recognize God's blessings on us as well. What a promise!

Even though greed is often thought of as relating primarily to money, it goes far deeper than that. We can have greed in our hearts for almost anything. Another definition that God gave me is "greed is wanting more than we should have or more than our share." We may have enough, but we keep desiring more than we need just to have it. We are never satisfied with what we have. This can pertain to clothing, food, cars, houses, wealth, prestige, fame, recognition and a myriad of other things. We may have twenty dresses in our closet, five of which we may hardly wear, but we see another dress that we just have to have, even though we may not need or can afford it at the time. Another example is, we may attend a lunch buffet, and we have had our share of all the courses and are quite full. However, that last piece of pie was so good, we just have to have one more piece of pie. So we stuff ourselves until we are uncomfortable and end up with indigestion, all because we refuse to control our desire for more.

The way to guard our hearts from greed is to be content. We need to learn to be satisfied with what we have.

> Keep your lives free from the love of money and be content with what you have, because God has said, 'Never will I leave you; never will I forsake you.' So we say with confidence, 'The Lord is my helper; I will not be afraid. What can mere mortals do to me?'
>
> (Hebrews 13:5-6 NIV)

Speaking from experience, I had to learn to be content. From childhood, I loved to shop. I could go to the mall and shop for hours, grabbing up as much as I could. I always felt like I needed to have everything I saw. However, recently when I was cleaning out my closet for a benevolent event, I realized something interesting. After gathering a huge shopping bag of clothing in excellent condition, some I had hardly worn, this extraction did not even put a dent in my closet. It was then that I realized that I had more than enough clothing and shoes, and I decided to be satisfied with what I had and focus more on giving to others rather than hoarding things for myself. Therefore, another cure for greed is giving to those in need.

Guard your heart from insecurity

A Google search provided the meaning of insecurity as "uncertainty or anxiety about oneself; lack of confidence." I am certain that every one of us at some point has experienced insecurity, where we lack confidence in some area of our lives. The definition that God gave me for insecurity is "believing who we are or what we have is not good enough." When we are insecure we demonstrate a lack of confidence in God. We start to depend on our own natural abilities and trust in our natural attributes and expect them to successfully carry us in this race of life. However, there will come a point in time when, if what or who we are depending on is not God, we will falter and fail.

People who are insecure are constantly anxious and worrying about some aspect of their lives. This is because they put their trust in themselves, other people or things that cannot guarantee the results they are seeking. Instead of allowing God into the driver's seat of their lives, they sit in that seat which was intended for Him and Him alone. Because they are relying on their own strength, insecure people are always wondering if things will work out or go according to the way they planned.

The ground they are standing on is unstable because they are depending on self-effort. Many times they are disappointed because things don't work out the way they envisioned. Therefore, they almost always expect to be disappointed because they believe it's just a matter of time before everything around them will come crumbling down. Because they have experienced disappointment, loss or betrayal of some sort, they begin to expect it or look for it even when it isn't there. Sound familiar or like someone you know?

I have suffered at the hands of insecurity. After being raped, I started to expect something bad to happen and have often looked for the next catastrophe. I have spent many years holding my breath and bracing myself for the worst, thinking that if I anticipate it and see it coming, the impact it would have on my life will not be as harsh and devastating. The problem with this plan is that I placed myself in the driver's seat and sought to be my own guardian angel, when God already dispatched guardian angels to protect me. I tried to cover myself, when Jesus already shed His blood to cover and protect me. So the more I tried and tried to keep watch over every aspect of my life, the more wound up and frustrated I became because I always came up short in my own strength. Therefore, I am now learning how to stop the balancing act by releasing my inhibitions and anxieties to God, Who already has the answers to my "challenges", both seen and unseen.

Another sign of insecurity is when we see other people's success, accomplishments, looks, relationships, professions, height, weight, possessions, etc. as a threat to ours. We begin to feel inadequate with who we are or what we have instead of seeing what we have as a gift from God. There will always be someone smarter, rich, better looking, taller, slimmer (or better developed), and appearing to be more successful than us, if we look around. But what is success? Success for us is fulfilling the call of God for our lives. Therefore all of us can be super successful if we yield to His plan and run our own race.

If we take the focus off of others, and begin to use the gifts, resources and attributes we have been blessed with, we would begin to see and appreciate how much God loves us and the amazing plan He has for our lives will be revealed. Our security would be found in God alone and we will begin to live fulfilled lives because we are running our race and accomplishing His will for our lives, relying fully on His strength and empowerment to get the job done.

Therefore guarding our hearts from insecurity will require surrendering everything to God, trusting and putting our confidence fully in Him and not our own natural abilities. Ephesians 6:10 tells us to "be strong in the Lord and in the power of His might." We must be secure in God, relying on His strength and choosing to see everyone's attributes including ours as a gift from God, given to fulfill a specific purpose. When all of us work together, using these gifts to the honor and glory of God, we will collectively accomplish God's mission on earth. Let's determine to daily recall all of God's blessings in our lives and in the lives of those around us and begin to celebrate each and every one.

Choose to focus on the blessings and forget the sorrows. Choose to focus on the goodness of God and forget the "so-called" shortcomings and soon they will be swallowed up in the strength that only God can give. God further admonishes us to allow Him to be our "confidence, and (he) shall keep (our) foot from being taken" (Proverbs 3:26). This is a promise of being planted on the solid rock of God and not the shakiness of our own strength. Then and only then will we have the power to overcome and endure in our race.

Another powerful promise is found in Proverbs:

> In the fear of the Lord is strong confidence: and his children shall have
> a place of refuge. (Proverbs 14:26)

When we reverence the Lord and His plans for our lives, He will be our confidence and provide us with the protection we long for and need. So we can choose to abandon our attempts to hold everything together ourselves, and "cast our cares on God, because He cares for us" (1 Peter 5:7).

Guard your heart from jealousy

I truly believe that insecurity in a lot of cases can lead to jealousy. This is because when we feel like what we have is not good enough, we may begin to look around and see others whom we "perceive" have what we should have. If we focus on the "strength" of others and then look at our perceived weaknesses and lack, we can begin to covet these things and become jealous of those who have them.

Freedictionary.com defines jealousy as "being envious or resentful of the achievement of others". We see others as having something good or desirable or achieving something terrific and we are unhappy about the fact that they have or did it and wish it was us instead of them. We ask ourselves, "Why couldn't that have happened to us?" instead of celebrating their success. The definition God gave me for jealousy is simply "wanting what other people have." Can any of us truly say we have never been jealous?

Jealousy is very dangerous and we should guard our hearts from it at all costs. This is because jealousy if not dealt with, will often lead to hatred, strife and, in some cases, murder. If we look all the way back to the first murder ever committed, it was committed because of jealousy. Cain, Adam and Eve's oldest son, killed his brother Abel because he was jealous of God's acceptance of his gifts. In Genesis 3 we learn that both Cain and Abel brought offerings to God. For some reason, Abel's offering was accepted and Cain's offering was not. This caused Cain to burn with jealousy towards his brother instead of looking inwardly to see why his gift was not accepted. God saw the condition of Cain's heart and addressed him:

> Then the Lord said to Cain, Why are you angry? Why is your face downcast? If you do what is right, will you not be accepted? But if you do not do what is right, sin is crouching at your door; it desires to have you, but you must rule over it. (Genesis 4:6-7 NIV)

God saw the jealousy and hatred building up in his heart, so He reached out to Cain asking him to consider his ways. However, Cain chose to act on the jealousy within and murdered his brother in cold blood. He saw Abel as the source of his problem, instead of looking within even after God had pointed it out. This is what can happen to us as well if we refuse the Lord's warning to guard our hearts against jealousy. Do you know how many people have been killed all because of jealousy?

Another biblical story in Genesis also easily portrays what can happen if jealousy is allowed to poison the heart. In Genesis 37, we find the story of Joseph. Joseph lived with his father, Jacob, along with his brothers in the land of Canaan. Jacob had given Joseph a coat of many colors and his brothers became jealous of him because of this gift. He also relayed his dream to his brothers of them bowing down to him and this caused them to be incensed with him. As a result, when they had him alone, they plotted to murder him and claim that a wild animal had devoured him. Thankfully, one of his brothers, Reuben, knew this was wrong and got them to alter their plans. However, when Reuben was absent they sold Joseph to an Ishmaelite caravan.

It's natural to become jealous of someone's gifts, attributes and favor. Therefore, all of us at any point in time can come face to face with jealousy as Cain or Joseph's brothers did.

> What leads to [the unending] quarrels and conflicts among you? Do they not come from your [hedonistic] desires that wage war in your [bodily] members [fighting for control over you]? You are jealous and covet [what others have] and your lust goes unfulfilled; so you murder. You are envious and cannot obtain [the object of your envy]; so you fight and battle. You do not have because you do not ask [it of God].
>
> (James 4:1-2)

James tells us that fights and quarrels among us occur because we allow our flesh, our natural desires, to want everything we see, even if it belongs to others. We allow ourselves to be overpowered by what we want and these desires spiral out of control and we become like a runaway train or a bull in a china store. This leads to us lashing out at and fighting with each other. The end result is jealousy, hatred and murder (in the context of the above verse).

To guard our hearts from jealousy, we have a choice to make. We don't have to willingly surrender to evil desires to have other people's things and the jealousy that results. We can choose God's way, which is to rejoice with others when they are blessed. Romans 12:15 says, "Rejoice with those who rejoice." When those around us are rejoicing because something good has happened in their lives, we ought to join in the celebration and rejoice with them with the same passion as if it were happening to us. If we make a determination to reject our selfish nature to want to have it all, and embrace the opportunity to applaud the success and accomplishment of others, then we know our hearts are in the right place – in the center of God's will. There will be nothing clogging or preventing God's love, purpose and Word to bear fruit in our lives.

We can also guard our hearts from jealousy, by delighting ourselves in the Lord. Psalm 37:4 encourages us to "delight thyself also in the Lord; and He shall give thee the desires of thine heart." Dictionary. com defines delight as both "to give great pleasure; and please highly" as well as "to have great pleasure or take great pleasure". It can be said then, that when we delight ourselves in the Lord, we give Him great pleasure and please Him highly by the things we do and the way we live. He then takes great pleasure in us and gives us our heart's desires. Why? Because when He finds pleasure in our lives, then He knows our hearts are in the right place and we can be trusted to have its desires. He knows that when He blesses us, we will not be selfish and use the blessings just for ourselves, but we will look around and reach out to fulfill His purpose and run a commendable, unselfish race.

What is the condition of your heart?

We must all look deep within ourselves to see if there is anything that is blocking the flow of God's anointing in our lives. Many times these things are so subtle that they go undetected. We know we are not enjoying all the benefits of the life that Jesus died to give us, but we are puzzled as to why. We need to check out the condition of our hearts and make sure that there are no undercurrents impeding our race. We can't run a healthy race without a healthy heart. We may be able to run for a while, but not for long. Take a moment and check your spiritual heart.

Remember to "Keep (guard) thy heart with all diligence; for out of it are the issues of life."

CHAPTER 9

RUN THE RACE WITH PATIENCE

Many of us may be destined to run a marathon rather than a one hundred meter dash. If we are to be successful in completing the work God has given us to do, we must pace ourselves. Challenges to our faith to endure will arise at every turn of the journey. Therefore, we have to develop the fruit of patience so that we can endure whatever comes our way.

When we are serving God with passion and perseverance, we are bound to run into ambushes intentionally set up to throw us off course. Trials, tragedies and wilderness experiences strike everyone and often without warning. We may feel that we are doing everything we are supposed to be doing, and all of a sudden things start to go haywire. The challenges tend to leave us wondering what's going on or where we went wrong. We literally feel like we have been knocked off of our feet and caught completely off guard.

I remember when I returned home from college in Canada in 1994, I was ready to soar and take the world by storm. However, as I mentioned earlier, a mere nine days later, I found myself being abducted, blindfolded, raped and violated by a group of men, shot twice and left for dead. This event happened without warning and I was left reeling and trying to make sense of what was going on. However, God kept me and brought me through victoriously and I am forever grateful. It was a painful experience and I had to be patient as God restored my dignity, self-respect, peace and faith little by little. It took time. Through this experience, I realized that the race I had set for myself was quite different from the one God had intended for me to run. As the years went by, I began to understand the call God had on my life to help hurting people heal. This storm in my life helped to blow away some things that were not helpful to my purpose and also put some things in divine order in my life. Sometimes, storms can be beneficial, as they remove the clutter and refuse from our lives, leaving behind only what is absolutely necessary for us to press on.

Jesus is in the boat

I recall the account in Mark's gospel of when Jesus and His disciples were in a boat destined to get to the other side. This story is recorded in chapter 4:35-41. He had been teaching all day and it was time to leave that place and minister to others across the lake and beyond. The disciples leaving to go to the other side can be compared to us running our race (fulfilling our God-ordained purpose). Like the storm the disciples experienced, we too will experience storms as we move towards the other side to accomplish the will of God for our lives. Storms are simply a part of life. However, we are unique like the disciples because as Christians, we always have Jesus in our boat. This assures us of victory.

It says in verse 37, "A furious squall came up, and the waves broke over the boat, so that it was nearly swamped. Jesus was in the stern, sleeping on a cushion." When the storm arose, Jesus was sleeping and it did not disturb His rest, so why should the disciples become alarmed? The King of kings was in their boat and He was sleeping as calm as a lamb, therefore they should have been calm as well knowing that Jesus is all powerful and would restore peace at the right time. They had seen Him heal Peter's mother-in-law of a fever. They were witnesses to Him healing the paralyzed man. They had been there when He healed the many sick and demon-possessed who had been brought to Him. All of these miracles had taken place in the first three chapters of Mark's gospel. Why would He now stop short of yet another miracle: calming the storm in their lives in chapter 4? He wouldn't!

Jesus was asleep which meant He was in a position of rest and peace. The disciples mistook His silence for inactivity, indifference and an unwillingness to act or respond to their current crisis. So they woke Him up thinking, "Maybe He just isn't aware!" Jesus arose, rebuked the wind and the waves, with the words, "Peace, be still" and immediately all became calm again.

Isn't it the same with us when we go through trials and God seems silent? We become afraid and forget about God's omnipresence, omnipotence and omniscience to stand up at the right time to rebuke the storms we face as we run this race, and restore calm and divine order in our lives. All we need is one word from God, "Peace, be still" and the storms in our lives will cease. When storms arise in our lives, we need answers and we search for them in every direction. As Christians, we expect to get our answers from God. But what happens when God appears to be quiet or asleep and there seems to be no apparent word forthcoming on what direction to take?

One person who I believe experienced the silence of God in his life during a difficult period was Job. The story of his life in told in the 42 chapters of his book in the Old Testament. In one day Job went from being the richest man in the world to losing it all. He lost his oxen, donkeys, sheep, camels and his ten children. The next day, he went from perfect health to being covered with boils. All of this happened to Job without warning. Job didn't get a heads-up, saying "everything is going to be okay.....this is just a test. You will be fine." No, rather there was divine "silence".

There are numerous lessons we can learn from the story of Job that can help us to exercise patience and respond properly to the challenges we face when there seems to be no "divine directives".

Focus on the good God has already done

After Job lost everything, he was still able to focus on the positive. He said, "Naked I came from my mother's womb and naked I shall return, The Lord gave and The Lord has taken away. Blessed be the Name of The Lord." Job still acknowledged that every blessing he had enjoyed throughout his life was from God and therefore God was still worthy of praise. He found the "things to praise God for". He had a relationship with God and in spite of the difficulties he still stood and praised God.

When we face trials, do we cry out in praise to God or do we cry out in disappointment and despair? If we have been spending time with God in prayer and reading His Word, our response should be, "Lord, I don't understand what is going on, but, I know You and I know You are sovereign and in control of my life, so I choose to rejoice." Like the psalmist we declare:

> I will bless The Lord at all times and His praise shall continually be in my mouth. (Psalm 34:1)

We have to learn to magnify or make great The Lord in every situation, even in the midst of calamity and tragedy. It may be hard but if we take the first step of opening our mouths in praise, we will experience God's supernatural power in our lives to take us safely over to the other side.

Resist the urge to blame or curse God

After Job's second test when his body broke out in sores, his wife told him to give up and throw in the towel by "cursing God and dying." Now his wife had enjoyed all the best of God's blessings when Job was prosperous. However, when the rough times came she was ready to throw in the towel. Personally, I think she was speaking from a place of brokenness, after she had just lost all of her children as well. She may not have been at the place in her relationship with God where Job was. Job had to, therefore, bring her back into reality by saying, "You are talking like a foolish woman, shall we accept good from God and not trouble?" Even when the person closest to him was encouraging him to give up, Job's faith and perseverance still prevailed. He remained patient!

God knew what was in Job. He knew that Job would be able to endure the trials he was facing. Others may not have made it through but Job made it because his trust was in God. Likewise, God knows us better than we know ourselves. He knows exactly how much we can bear. Therefore, when we face difficulties, we already possess the power and persistence to "press toward the mark" and overcome the obstacles. Even if God doesn't say a word, He never leaves us and knows just how much we can bear and will not let us go under but will rather take us over!

So we need to mind our mouths in the trial and be careful to speak life!

Distance yourself from negativity

Job had three friends who came to visit him when they heard of all of his misfortunes. Job, in his broken state, allowed these companions to speak evil of him, trying to convince him that what he was going through was a result of some sin he had committed. However, we know from Job 1 that Job was righteous and it was because of his righteous standing with God that Satan asked to test him to see if his relationship with God was fair-weathered or genuine. These verses relay the exchange between God and Satan concerning Job:

> Then the Lord said to Satan, 'have you considered my servant Job? There is no one on earth like him; he is blameless and upright, a man who fears God and shuns evil.' 'Does Job fear God for nothing', Satan replied. 'Have You not put an hedge around him and his household and everything he has? You have blessed the work of his hands, so that his flocks and herds are spread throughout the land. But now stretch out your hand and strike everything he has, and he will surely curse you to your face.' (Job 1:8-11 NIV)

So Job's test came as a result of his right living.

People often assume that tragedy is a result of sin, but there are many people who have suffered even though they have done nothing wrong. Jesus tells us:

> I am the true vine, and my Father is the gardener. He cuts off every branch in me that bears no fruit, while every branch that bears fruit He prunes so that it will be even more fruitful. (John 15:1-2 NIV)

Therefore, we will sometimes get cut no matter what state we are in. If we claim to be righteous and are fruitless, we will be cut off. If we are righteous and fruitful, we will be cut through pruning. Dictionary. com defines pruning as "to cut or lop superfluous or undesired twigs, branches, or roots from; trim." So as producing members of the Body of Christ, we are occasionally trimmed to ensure that all of the unnecessary twigs are removed so that we can be even more fruitful for God.

Job's friends said they came to bring him comfort, but instead they brought him condemnation. They condemned him for some sin they assumed he had committed. Who were they to condemn him? We may experience the same treatment as we attempt to run our race. When we experience difficulties, there may be some with judgmental eyes. However, Romans 8:1 assures us that "there is now therefore no condemnation for us who are in Christ Jesus, those who walk after the Spirit and not the flesh".

We have to learn to stay as far away as possible from people who discourage us instead of encourage us when we face obstacles and disappointments. These are the ones who can deepen our wounds especially when God seems silent. There will be times when we will have to encourage ourselves in the Lord, and not depend on others to do it for us.

Psalm 30:5 declares, "Weeping may endure for a night, but joy cometh in the morning." No matter how long the night may seem, morning has to eventually come and with its arrival we are guaranteed God's joy. Job would have been better off if he had sent those "so-called friends" away and continued to focus on the faithfulness of God. Likewise, we also have to be careful not to solicit or encourage the advice of "doomsayers dressed in friend's clothing." Some may mean well, but they are just giving their diagnosis based on what they think are the facts (that is what they can see) and not on faith. 2 Corinthians 5:7 says, "For we walk by faith, not by sight."

Job was standing strong until his friends came to access the situation. That is why it is imperative that we choose our friends wisely, especially those who are in our inner circle, those who are close to our ears. There is a well-known saying, "friends are like elevators. They either take you up or bring you down."

Similarly, when we go through trials, there may not be a physical voice that we hear, but rather voices in our heads that condemn us. They may be whispering to us, "God is punishing you" or "This is happening because of something you did". This is the time to look within ourselves and evaluate whether or not we are living according to God's precepts. If we discover that there is an area in our lives that needs God's healing touch, then we need to remember that there is forgiveness in Jesus, make the necessary changes and continue to run our course for God's glory. However, many times these mental allegations are unfounded and if this is found to be the case, then we have to "cast down imaginations and everything that exalts itself above the knowledge of God, and take every thought captive" (2 Corinthians 10:5). How do we still these thoughts when God seems silent?

Meditate on the Word of God

Many times we choose the advice of a friend over the Word of God. This is why we end up with a lot of "corrupt communication" when we are in the difficult places of life. Even if we feel God is distant, His

Word is just a Bible away. In these highly technological times, we have easy access to God's Word on our computers, laptops, iPads, iPods and cell phones. We can spend less time searching for that new dress, pair of shoes or the latest technological gadget and more time reading God's Word and discovering His next steps for our lives.

Hebrews 4:12 says, "The Word of God is living and active." It is still powerful after all these years. When the Word is spoken over our circumstances, it breathes life into us. I can testify that there has not been a time when I was down and out that after reading the Word of God, I did not get an injection of faith in my situation that empowered me to press on. When we have a problem, the Word of God needs to be a first response and not our last resort. It is quite sad that many times we tend to leave God's solution for the last, and only after we have tried everything else and failed, we are willing to give God's way a "try".

I remember when I was locked in the trunk of a car after being abducted, it was the living and active Word of God that I uttered out of my mouth that saved my life. In that trunk, "I called on the Lord Who is worthy to be praised and I was saved from my enemies" (Psalm 18:3 NIV). I began to declare the Word of God in my midnight hour. I said, "No weapon formed against me shall prosper", which is found in Isaiah 54:17 and "when the enemy shall come in like a flood the Spirit of the Lord will lift up a standard against him", found in Isaiah 59:19. A weapon had been formed against me, namely a gun and the enemy did come in like a flood when I was forced into a canal even though I could not swim. However, I am ecstatic to report that the living and active Word of God coming out of my mouth squashed the plans of the enemy to bring me death and destruction. Hallelujah!

In order to be able to call on God's Word in times of trouble, we have to study it daily and meditate on it day and night. Psalm 1:3 assures us that the person who does this will "be like a tree planted by streams of water, which yields its fruit in season and whose leaf does not wither – whatever they do prospers." Therefore, it does not matter how dry it may look in any area of our lives, God's Word in us will cause us to prosper and have great success. However, we cannot wait until the battle rages for us to become students of the Word of God. The Word is the blueprint for our lives. Therefore, when a situation arises in our lives, we will be conversant enough in the Word of God that we know where to go for our answers. We must continue to stand during the difficult times of life knowing that our breakthrough and deliverance is on the way and will come in right on time. We are assured that:

> This vision message is a witness pointing to what is to come. It can hardly wait. It doesn't lie. It's on the way. It will come in right on time.
> (Habakkuk 2:2 MSG)

To say that God's vision and good plan for our lives can hardly wait, means that it is ready to burst forth into our lives.

Remember... you are serving God

In the story of Job, even though God boasted to Satan about Job being one of His finest servants, there appeared to be silence in Heaven as Job's situation went from bad to worse. Job's friends had certainly compounded the problem, but it was in the midst of this back and forth exchange that Job began to remember the God he served.

> I know my Redeemer lives and in the end He shall stand upon the earth. And after my skin has been destroyed, yet in my flesh, I will see God. I will see Him with my own eyes - I, and not another. How my heart yearns within me. (Job 19:25 NIV)

Job was yearning to see God and receive his vindication. He realized that God had not left him, but was very much alive in his life. His confidence in God's ability and willingness to show up in his situation, rescue and vindicate him had begun to return.

> Though He slay me, yet will I hope in Him. I will defend my ways to His face. Indeed, it will turn out for my deliverance. (Job 13:15 NIV)

What faith and determination Job demonstrated even in the midst of what he perceived as God's silence. He still found the strength to trust God even when he couldn't trace Him.

We must, likewise, display the same tenacity and perseverance when we face obstacles and experience God's so-called silence. As we press on, let us remember what God says to us through Jeremiah:

> For I know what I am doing. I have it all planned out, plans to take care of you, not to abandon you, plans to give you the future you hope for. (Jeremiah 29:11 MSG)

God wants to give us the future that we are hoping for. What are you hoping for today? Most people hope for provision, good health, peace of mind, healthy relationships and a purpose for living. God has promised us who are a part of His family that it is His plan to give us these things. God says that the ride may be a little bumpy right now, but our final destination is to the place we've been hoping for. So be patient and keeping running!

God can turn your situation around

Like Job, we have to call to remembrance all God has already done for us. When we feel down and out, let us reflect again and again on this scripture:

> I remember my affliction and my wandering, the bitterness and the gall. I well remember them, and my soul is downcast within me. Yet this I call to mind and therefore I have hope: because of the Lord's great love we are not consumed, for his compassions never fail. They are new every morning; great is your faithfulness. I say to myself, "the Lord is my portion: Therefore I will wait for Him.
>
> (Lamentations 3:19-24 NIV)

God's compassions are new every morning; therefore we don't have to depend on yesterday's compassion. When morning comes, there is new hope, new compassion and a new reason for living. We can make it through another day because there is a fresh supply of grace from God. This grace is enough to take us through the day and we don't have to save some for tomorrow because our God is big enough and powerful enough to provide us with all the grace we need when we need it. It reminds me of the manna that God provided for the children of

Israel when they were in the wilderness. They were told not to store the manna because God was their Provider who would give them fresh manna every morning. The Lord's Prayer even says, "Give us this day our daily bread" (Matthew 6:11). What a mighty God we serve, that every day we get new mercy, grace and everything we need to make it through another day.

In Psalm 27:13, King David also testified of the goodness of God when he penned, "I am still confident of this: I WILL see the goodness of the Lord in the land of the living. Wait for the Lord, be strong and take heart. Wait I say on the Lord." Can we, even though we face many troubles, still have the confidence that David displayed knowing that at the end of the trial there is a place of goodness prepared just for us? I believe that Job knew this as well. Let this be our testimony from this moment on: no matter how far downhill we may go, we are fully convinced we will experience God's goodness before we close our eyes.

King David again encouraged us in Psalm 23:6 where it is written, "Surely goodness and mercy will follow me all the days of my life." Can you imagine that, living every day with goodness and mercy as your travelling companions? David is so confident that this was going to happen he prefixes it with the word "surely" which dicitionary.com says means "undoubtedly, assuredly, or certainly" – in essence it will happen! Just before this verse in Psalm 23, David talked about his enemies and how God "preparest a table before him in the presence of his enemies." That is why we don't have to be concerned about our enemies, because whenever they are present, God shows up and prepares a table before us in their very presence.

According to this psalm, God also "anoints our heads with oil and our cups runneth over" with blessings. God's favor follows us wherever we go and doors will begin to open because we depend on God's faithfulness and refuse to give up. We have to press through our trials to get to the triumphs!

Accept God's rebuke

Job had allowed his friends to go too far and as a result he began to question the God he served, the One who had blessed him and always provided for him. God allowed the exchange between him and his friends to go on for 37 chapters. Then He began to confront Job about the things he had said. This is why it is so important to guard our ear gates and be careful whom we allow to speak into our situations, to ensure that we don't receive the "corrupt communication" I referred to earlier. When we allow people around us to confess gloom and doom we are susceptible to what they confess. This would be the ideal time to put on our "spiritual earphones" and listen to what God is saying to us. Even though He seems silent, if we listen carefully, He is always saying something to guide us, either through His Word or some other means.

When I was going through a period of physical challenges, which led to emotional and mental instability, my husband would always tell me to "change the channel of my mind" from negative thinking to positive, God centered thinking. So when the message is "corrupt" change the channel, by reading the Word of God or an encouraging book, or by praying or doing something good for others. Change the focus of your thinking and your outlook will change as well.

When we get caught up in other people's opinions over the Word of God, God will arise and remind us Who He is in our lives. In Chapter 38 of Job, God began to question Job saying, "Then the Lord spoke to Job out of the storm:

> Who is this that obscures my plans with words without knowledge? Brace yourself like a man; I will question you, and you shall answer me. "Where were you when I laid the earth's foundation? Tell me, if you understand. Who marked off its dimensions? Surely you know! Who stretched a measuring line across it? (Job 38:2-5 NIV)

This was God's way of asking Job, "Don't you remember Who I AM? I AM the Creator of the Universe and I AM the One Who put everything in its place. I AM the Great I AM and I AM in control of your situation." God had to remind Job of Who He was and what He had already done and was still capable of doing in his life!

Similarly, God will remind us of Who is He is, always has been and will forever be to us when we begin to doubt and question Him when faced with challenges.

Expect God to act

It's imperative to remember that it is not God's intent for us to live a life of misery. We must dismiss that out of our minds if we expect to run a successful race. God will act at the right time and turn our challenges around for our good.

> In all things we know that God works for the good of those who love
> Him and are called according to His purpose. (Romans 8:28 NIV)

It says that we KNOW, which means we are fully convinced without a shadow of doubt. Next, I want to emphasize that it says ALL things, which means the good things and the bad, difficult, disappointing and challenging things, God will work out in our best interests. In verse 37 of the same chapter, Paul goes on to assure us that "in all these situations (the good, the bad and he ugly), we are more than conquerors through Christ Jesus." This is our guarantee that if we wholly trust, believe and hold on to God no matter what may be happening in our lives, we have the power to overcome the obstacles we face by the power of God. Then Paul wraps up the end of the chapter in verse 38 with the comforting words that "nothing is able to separate us from the love of God." The trials we encounter cannot stop God from loving us.

What does God's love for us motivate Him to do? It motivates Him to act mightily on our behalf and restore divine order to our lives.

This is what happened with Job. God completely restored him by giving him double of all of the assets he had lost and just as many children as he had before. I believe that He will do the same for us as

His children. He will restore all of the assets we may have lost along the way and give us double blessings. However, it requires patience and the ability to endure. This scripture shows how Job's patience paid off:

> As you know, we count as blessed those who have persevered. You have heard of Job's perseverance and have seen what the Lord finally brought about. The Lord is full of compassion and mercy. (James 5:11)

The prophet Joel says it like this:

> "I will repay you for the years the locusts have eaten – the great locust and the young locust, the other locusts and the locust swarm – my great army that I sent among you. You will have plenty to eat, until you are full, and you will praise the name of the LORD your God, who has worked wonders for you; never again will my people be shamed.
>
> (Joel 2:25-26 NIV)

We are engrafted in the family of God because of our relationship with Jesus. Not only will we receive double for the trouble we faced, but we will also be able to enjoy these blessings as well. His promise to us is everlasting joy as we walk through and come out of the fires of life.

> The Lord blessed Job at the end of his life more than at the beginning.
>
> (Job 42:12)

This is so encouraging to know, because Job's life was already blessed at the beginning, and many of us would have been quite satisfied with that. However, God's plans for Job did not stop there. He wanted to give Job the future that he was hoping for. He wants to do the same for us. Will you let Him guide you through your trials and bring you to the place you have been hoping for?

Repent, forgive and pray for those who have hurt us

Job repented for doubting God's love and concern for him when his life fell apart:

> Job answered God: "I'm convinced: You can do anything and everything. Nothing and no one can upset your plans. You asked,

'Who is this muddying the water, ignorantly confusing the issue, second-guessing my purposes?' I admit it. I was the one. I babbled on about things far beyond me, made small talk about wonders way over my head. You told me, 'Listen, and let me do the talking. Let me ask the questions. You give the answers.' I admit I once lived by rumors of you; now I have it all firsthand – from my own eyes and ears! I'm sorry – forgive me. I'll never do that again, I promise! I'll never again live on crusts of hearsay, crumbs of rumor." (Job 42:1-6 MSG)

What an awesome, sincere prayer of repentance! Job admitted that he realized that he had only known God from a distance, just from the rumors that he had heard. However, after his wilderness experience, he finally knew God intimately and realized how much He truly loved him. Things had always gone well for Job, therefore he assumed that God loved him, but when things fell apart for him and he had to hold on to God's love and words for dear life, his spiritual eyes were opened and exposed to the love of God firsthand, up close and personal.

We must repent as well for the times we doubted God's sovereignty because we were blinded by suffering. It is time to allow the fires in our lives to bring us closer and more intimately acquainted with the God above all gods, who is indeed our loving Heavenly Father. Next, we must determine to forgive those who have hurt us along the way, like Job did. These people may be close to us. They may even be people in our inner circle. Forgive them and let the bitterness and resentment go, and watch God turn your captivity around just as He did for Job. Forgiveness always precedes restoration and blessings.

As we conclude this chapter, let's do a recap. Job's tragedy began in chapter 1. It was a whirlwind of troubles out of seemingly nowhere and God appeared silent for 37 chapters. We don't know how long this trial lasted in terms of time, but we know that however long it was, it seemed too long for Job. Similarly, no matter how long our trials last, it always seems too long for us to bear. It can be compared to when there is a power outage. If the power is off for five minutes, it seems like that is the longest five minutes of our lives, especially if it is at night time when we can't see anything or if it happens in the middle of our favorite television program.

The cocoon is not your final destination

I have learned that going through a trial when God appears silent is similar to a caterpillar going through the metamorphic change of a cocoon on its way to a butterfly (the final destination or the future it is hoping for) – which is the position of soaring. What is interesting is the caterpillar doesn't know the cocoon is coming. It just keeps walking around doing its thing until one day everything suddenly becomes dark and it realizes it can't move. It's trapped! Isn't that similar to how we feel when confronted with a challenge and God seems so quiet. Both processes are dark and lonely but they are necessary to get to the next level – the level of soaring. In the cocoon we will feel alone. It will be dark and God may appear absent. However, His apparent silence doesn't mean He is not there behind the scenes working out something great for us. We still experience His grace and mercy every step of the way. He is still our provider and sustainer.

During our time of incubation, He may not allow anybody to help us, just like that developing butterfly. This is the time God is allowing our spiritual muscles to develop to gain the strength necessary to soar. If He permits someone to assist us at this crucial stage of development, it would be to our spiritual detriment because we need to strengthen our wings. So, He places us in a position where we have to use them to push through the resistance of the cocoon so our wings can become strong enough to propel us through the winds, clouds and storms of life into the bright sunshine that awaits us after the rain. Therefore, we are strengthened in the struggle. We may experience resistance in this race we face, but it all contributes to the building up of our spiritual stamina to endure to the end and get to the place we have been hoping to reach. It is there we receive our prize from God Himself for completing our course!

Let us remember to stay faithful to God in the midst of our trials and continue to run our race with diligence; leaving the difficulties in the hands of our caring Heavenly Father Who has "every detail of our lives worked into something good!"

> Why would you ever complain, O Jacob, or, whine, Israel, saying, "God has lost track of me. He doesn't care what happens to me"? Don't you know anything? Haven't you been listening? God doesn't come and go. God lasts. He's Creator of all you can see or imagine. He doesn't get tired out, doesn't pause to catch his breath. And he knows everything, inside and out. He energizes those who get tired, gives fresh strength to dropouts. For even young people tire and drop out, young folk in their prime stumble and fall. But those who wait upon God get fresh strength. They spread their wings and soar like eagles, they run and don't get tired, they walk and don't lag behind. (Isaiah 40:27-31 MSG)

These verses assure us that God has not forgotten us. He knows what we are going through, isn't caught off guard by our challenges, never leaves us and doesn't get tired. He will give us fresh strength for each challenge we face and we WILL be able to stand, walk, run and SOAR if we wait on His strength, power and deliverance in our lives. What a blessed assurance!

Job, even with all of his success, at the start was just a caterpillar! He was still in seed form. Imagine that! With all he had, that still was not God's desired end for his life. God wanted to give him double but he had to go through the process of the cocoon to get to the life God had prepared for him.

I encourage you not to despise your cocoon but see it for what it is: a passageway to your destiny, the place you have been hoping for and God's ordained place of double blessings in your life!

CHAPTER 10

LEAVE YOUR WORRIES WITH GOD

*E*very day the enemy aims his fiery darts in our direction to throw us off course, to distract us for a while, or to try to stop us from running our race completely. It may come in various forms. The more mature we become in God, the less likely he will be able to distract us with the "overt sins".

We may keep all of the Ten Commandments. However, what about the subtle things he uses to distract us, nagging questions and concerns such as: How will this bill get paid? When will my child get serious about God? I don't have enough time to get everything done at home. The house is a mess! What have I accomplished in life so far? When will I be able to afford a new car or home? When will I get a steady job? When will I get that well deserved promotion?

There are a whole host of thoughts that try to invade our minds just like bacteria tries to poison a cell in our bodies. I believe worry is the spiritual infection we contract when we allow spiritual bacteria to infiltrate our minds.

Jesus' answer to worry

What does God have to say about worry? He simply says, "Don't do it". Jesus commands us not to worry three times in the following passage:

> Therefore, I tell you, <u>do not worry</u> about your life, what you will eat or drink; or your body, what you will wear. Is not life more than food, and the body more than clothes? Look at the birds of the air; they do not sow or reap or store away into barns, and yet your Heavenly Father feeds them. Are you not more valuable than they? Can any one of you by worrying add a single hour to your life? And why do you worry about clothes? See how the flowers of the field grow. They do not labor or spin. Yet I tell you not even Solomon in all his splendor was dressed like one of these. If that is how God clothes the grass of the field, which is here today and tomorrow is thrown into the fire, will He not much more clothe you—you of little faith? So <u>do not worry</u>, saying, 'What shall we eat?' or 'What shall we drink?' or 'What shall we wear?' For the pagans run after all these things, and your heavenly Father knows that you need them. But seek first His kingdom and His righteousness, and all these things will be given to you as well. Therefore <u>do not worry</u> about tomorrow, for tomorrow will worry about itself. Each day has enough trouble of its own. (Matthew 6:25-34 NIV)

We must remember Who our ultimate Source is: the God Who is more than enough, Who owns the cattle on a thousand hills, and to Whom the earth and all its fullness belong. He is the El Shaddai God, the God Almighty of blessings. He is all-powerful, all-knowing and ever present. That's Who we serve. We say this and quote a lot of scriptures, but we still find ourselves worrying about tomorrow. I believe it is because we don't always seek God first. How many of us can say we seek God first all the time?

To be the overcomers and more than conquerors in the area of worry, we must seek God first every single time. This is Jesus' answer to worry according to this above scripture. Spending time with God is the answer to all of the worries, doubts and fears that plague us. In every situation we face, we ask God for His wisdom and guidance.

I have had a lot of experience with worry. I might add "more than my share". However, it wasn't always like that. Growing up, I could say I had a good life. All my needs were met. I basically got what I wanted, enjoyed my school life, went on vacations and lived in comfort. So basically I had nothing to worry about. Life was good!

Then in 1994, my "perfect" world was shattered when I was abducted and raped. I had no other human to defend me. The situation surrounding the attack was a bit questionable because I was on a beach at night with a friend. I was violated and almost died. Then a host of negative emotions including guilt, shame, un-forgiveness, and of course worry and fear flooded my soul.

The world as I knew it had been changed, and my perspective was altered as well. I became keenly aware that "bad things can happen" and more importantly "they can happen to me". I was a Christian at the time of this incident and God not only saved my life, but He began to heal me from the ravages of rape. Piece by piece, he restored me.

However, one area has been a constant struggle since then: Fear and the worry that followed closely behind. For years, I have struggled with chronic worry. If there was a Worrier's Anonymous", I should have enrolled. We hear a lot of Alcoholics Anonymous today. However, I believe there is an even bigger addiction that most of the population on this people planet battles with: WORRY!

If I were to take a poll today of how many of us are prone to worry, I believe it would probably be more than 75% of the world's population.

I began to research different people's interpretations and views on worry. Here are a few listed below:

Corrie ten Boom says, "Worry is carrying tomorrow's load with today's strength – carrying two days at once. It is moving into tomorrow ahead of time. Worrying doesn't empty tomorrow of its sorrow, it empties today of its strength."

I find this so interesting because it implies that when we worry, we are acting like a juggler trying to balance two different days with their numerous challenges in our two hands. Eventually something is going to fall and be destroyed. Instead of enjoying today and pressing through the situations that present themselves, we go all the way into tomorrow trying to solve problems that have not and may, in fact, never arise. Therefore, we will always feel worn out, because we haven't received the grace from God to face tomorrow's challenges as yet.

June Hunt says, "Worry is most often a prideful way of thinking that you have more control over life and its circumstances than you actually do".

Isn't this the truth? We feel if we worry we can actually find some solution to our problems. In essence, it is our duty to worry and mull over the situation. However, it always proves to be a lesson in futility because our worry produces nothing but stress in our lives, usually manifesting in our bodies as sickness.

I like Rick Warren's solution to worry, which is, "The more you pray, the less you'll panic. The more you worship, the less you worry. You'll feel more patient and less pressured."

Prayer and worship dispel panic and worry. So let's put this into practice. The next time a worrisome thought enters our minds, let's begin to worship God, pray to Him and see if that thought has a chance of survival.

What is worry? Worry is allowing the obstacles, challenges and setbacks we face drown out the voice of God in our lives. We know God is with us, but we don't really believe that He can and will help us when all hell breaks loose. So we think about and pine over our own solution to the problems or setbacks, instead of leaving them to the One "Who never leaves us or forsakes us" (Hebrews 12:5) and has been in our end and declared victory. Because God instructs us not to worry, when we choose to worry about a situation instead of placing it in the hands of God, we are actually committing a sin. We often focus on the "big" sins such as murdering, lying, cheating, stealing, but worry is just as much a sin as these and we have to resist the urge to worry, fret or doubt as we run our race.

Another personal definition of worry which is found in my first book *A Time to Heal: Restoration from the Ravages of Rape* is this: "Worry is meditating on the negative". Things look bad, and they may even be bad, so we roll all of the bad things over and over in our minds until they have formed a stronghold or a fortress and we don't even give God's Word and promises a chance to bear fruit in our situation. We don't make a determination to see what the Word says about our challenge and roll that over and over in our minds instead until God's Word becomes the stronghold of our life.

For me, facing danger or loss has been a big challenge. I think it is because of way back then, I thought I was going to die and so I became afraid. So anytime my family and I faced something that I perceived as danger, that old familiar feeling of fear or dread would rise up in me. Now, I'm still alive so obviously God saved me. So why do I fear or dread danger or loss when God has already shown me that He is more powerful than death?

I want to encourage you today to go against the grain of the natural inclination to fret or worry in your current situation, and to begin to focus on and recall the promises God has made to us in His Word. Let's remember Who God is to us.

God is our Perfect Protector

I've picked you. I haven't dropped you. Don't panic. I'm with you. There is no need to fear for I'm your God. I'll hold you steady, keep a firm grip on you. Count on it: Everyone who had it in for you will end up in the cold – real losers. Those who worked against you will end up empty-handed - nothing to show for their lives. When you go out looking for your old adversaries you won't find them – Not a trace of your old enemies, not even a memory. That's right. Because I, your God, have a firm grip on you and I'm not letting you go. I'm telling you, don't panic. I'm right here to help you. (Isaiah 41:9-13 MSG)

I want to re-visit the situation I referred to earlier. When I was abducted, I was blind folded and placed in the trunk of a car. The person I was with had already been shot, so I knew that a gun was present and the perpetrators had no problem using it. In the natural, I couldn't see how I would escape what appeared to be certain death. No one knew where I was, so how could I be rescued? I remembered the faithfulness of God in my life thus far and I began "to call upon the Lord". I cried out to Him and told Him that I needed Him to perform a mighty rescue operation in my life and that if He didn't show up that night, there would be no tomorrow for me. As I mentioned earlier, I reminded Him of His Word in Isaiah 54:17: "No weapon that is formed against me shall prosper" and in Isaiah 59:19 which says, "When the enemy shall come in like a flood, the Spirit of the Lord shall lift a standard against him." After I prayed about the situation, I had peace. This was not the time or place to have a meltdown or lose control. With the Lord's help, I remained peaceful and calm. I, like Paul, was waiting on a verdict – would I live or would I die?

There may be difficulties in this race of our lives but we have an Answer, a Hope, an Advocate and an Ever Present Help in the time of trouble. So our mindset should be, we refuse to worry, or become anxious but in every situation we face, we take our worries and concerns and leave them in the hands of the God with the plan for our lives. When we leave our worries in His hands, we do so with thankful hearts, knowing that He will hear us and work things out in our best interests. When we do this God makes us a promise: we are guaranteed that His peace will transcend our understanding. Dictionary.com defines transcend as "to go beyond or rise above the limits of" our understanding. This peace will guard our hearts and minds and keep them safe in Christ Jesus.

I can truly say that I experienced peace in the trunk of the car that night. I also experienced God's peace as they pulled me out of the car and dragged me through the bushes. I cannot say that fear was fully absent, but I know that God's peace in my life was bigger than the fear that was trying to break through. That is because I experienced the perfect protection of God throughout that entire ordeal. Even though I was shot at twice, each bullet missed me. Even though I was forced to fall into a deep canal and could not swim, I didn't drown! Isn't God great? I may have come out with a few scars, but I came out in my right mind and with an unshakable belief that God is a refuge, strength and shield!

We don't have to worry about anything, but we can choose to pray about everything. God is our Everything: our Provider, Protector, Peace and our Ever Present Help! We have to learn how "to leave our worries with God" as it admonishes us in 1 Peter 5:7. Why? Because "He cares for us" according to this verse.

Once in a small group I hosted in our home called "Faith for Trying Times", the Lord gave me an idea to create a "Leave our worries with God" piggy bank. Every week, we were challenged to place our concerns in the bank as a symbol that we were depositing them with God. Since this bank had no way of opening unless you cut it open, trying to take the worries back would be difficult and would require a lot of effort. This is a lesson for us. When we give our situations to God, we have to release them and let them go so that He can work something beautiful out of them. We relinquish our control and submit to His Divine solutions which are always far better than anything we could think or dream of on our own!

God is our Perfect Provider

If we live long enough, our situations will change. Some of the things we were able to do before, we may not be able to do now, maybe because we are either making less money or prices for necessities are skyrocketing. I am amazed when I go to the food store weekly, how an item that may have cost $3 last week now cost $4 and by the next week it is climbing up to $5. Sadly, paychecks don't increase weekly to accommodate the rising costs of living. It is natural to become concerned when you can no longer afford certain things.

The psalmist gives us God's assurance that He will provide us with everything we need.

> The blameless spend their days under the Lord's care, and their inheritance will endure forever. In times of disaster they will not wither; in days of famine they will enjoy plenty. I was young and now I am old, yet I have never seen the righteous forsaken or their children begging bread. They are always generous and lend freely; their children will be a blessing. (Psalm 37:18-19; 25-26 NIV)

No matter how bad things get in this world, God promises to provide for those who are His. This scripture confirms that not only will we be provided for, but also we will have plenty. Why will we have plenty? This will put us in a position to be a blessing to those who don't have and therefore introduce them to Jehovah Jireh, the Lord our Provider.

We can be naturally discontent because of our sinful nature. We want the best and want to be the best and anything less can really make us dissatisfied, especially if other people appear to be ahead of us. That is why Paul said in Philippians 4 that he learned the secret to being content. This means that although it does not come naturally to us, we can learn how to be content, we can train ourselves to be satisfied, just like we learn to talk or walk. It will hurt our flesh, because the flesh wants to have what it wants when it wants it.

However, we can and must learn to be grateful for what we have at the time, and trust God to provide what we need. This is what Paul did, and God saw his needs and touched the hearts of the Philippian church to send him a love gift. Paul declared that he rejoiced in the Lord. He was thankful that the Philippian church had sent the gift, but recognized that the real source was God.

God works through different channels to get His blessings to us. However, those people are only conduits. Your employer is only a conduit of God's blessings to you. If your place of employment closed down, God will open up another channel to get His blessings to you. When we focus on the real Source, we can be content because, we know that He will provide all of our needs. Paul rested in God and relied on Him for everything.

God is our Perfect Pioneer

Trust God from the bottom of your heart; don't try to figure out everything on your own. Listen for God's voice in everything you do, everywhere you go; He's the One who will keep you on track.

(Proverbs 3:5-6 MSG)

If we place our complete trust in God, He will be our lifelong travelling companion and our perfect pioneer in this race of life. He will navigate us through life's obstacles and challenges and "make us lie down in green pastures, lead us beside quiet waters, refresh our souls and lead us along the right paths for His Name's sake" according to Psalm 23:2-3. This happens because we allow the Lord to be the shepherd of our lives and we follow His leading. Verses 4-5 promises that our shepherd will be with us even when "we walk through the darkest valley, and we will fear no evil, because He is with us; His rod and staff comfort us." When God is near, we have nothing to fear!

The verses in Proverbs tell us: "don't try to figure out everything on our own. Listen for His voice in everything we do." In other words, God's got the master plan for our lives and if we would stop and listen to what He is saying, He will point us in the direction that leads to our purpose being fulfilled.

Sadly, many times, we want to go our own way and chart our own course. We want to be the "master of our own ship" and we usually end up in troubled waters that God did not intend for us to travel. King Solomon, the wisest man that ever lived, says it like this in Proverbs 14:12 and 16:25, "there is a way that seemeth wise unto a man, but in the end, thereof are the ways of death." There are some paths we may want to take that seem so enticing, that look like they will take us to God's destination for our lives (the place we have been hoping for), but they are "channels with false lighthouses" that can lead us to destruction. This is why it is all the more imperative that we seek God first and ask Him to be the captain and navigator of our journey to the place He has prepared for us.

God gives us perfect positioning

> We can lift up our eyes unto to the hills, from whence cometh our help. Our help cometh from the Lord, which made heaven and earth. He will not suffer our foot to be moved: He that keepeth us will not slumber. (Psalm 121:1-3)

When we look up to the Lord, and recognize that all of our help and strength comes from Him, we can know without a shadow of doubt that we shall not be moved or utterly cast down. We have perfect positioning in God. He keeps us steady on our feet as we run. Yes, sometimes we may stumble but we will land on our feet if we trust Him to uphold us. Psalm 37 assures us of this:

> The steps of a good man are ordered by the Lord: and He delighted in his way. Though he fall, he shall not be utterly cast down: for the Lord upholdeth him with His hand. (Psalm 37:23-24)

So, we are assured of God's divine "catch" when we trip on the rough patches of our course. It is comforting to know no matter how late it is or how dark the night is, God never sleeps and is always aware of what is going on in our lives.

God gives us perfect peace

I again recall when I was abducted. It was nighttime. While many slept, my life hung in the balance. But, God was awake, alert and on the job. He rescued me when others were asleep and did not even know I was missing and needed help. I can personally attest, that "He is the friend that sticketh closer than a brother" (Proverbs 18:24).

Earlier, I wrote about how I experienced God's peace in my life when I was placed in the trunk of a car after being abducted. Over the years, God's peace has sustained me in other situations as well. Recently, our eldest son took most of his Bahamas Junior Certificate Examinations a year early in grade eight. His goal was to get all A's in these exams and he studied diligently and also prayed and fasted. My husband and I believed with him that he would get the results he was hoping for.

When the results came out a few months later, he had gotten A's in all the subjects but one. He was disappointed because he knew he had done his best. I felt it for him. Quickly, the Lord spoke these words into my ears, "all things work together for the good of them that love the Lord and are called according to His purpose (Romans 8:28)." I told him not to worry because every disappointment works out for the best and God would bless him with something better. In his mind, he was thinking that he would not be recognized by the Ministry of Education because he had just missed the requirement of five A's in one sitting. I prayed and prayed about this because I didn't want my son to lose faith in the power of prayer and fasting and in God. Amazingly, I started to see the peace of God become evident in his life. He would pray asking God that if a mistake had been made with his B grade, that it would be discovered and corrected. He would end by saying "but if not, I accept it and I am satisfied." He was fourteen and I was amazed by the mature view he took of this. When he returned to school for the new school year, he congratulated all of his friends who had received the 5 'A' requirement. He learned how to experience the peace of God in disappointments, something we adults struggle with daily (myself included).

As I prayed about this situation, God would whisper, "this is a later lesson, I will show you what I will do." So I waited, and eventually I allowed the peace of God to "keep my heart and mind safe in Christ Jesus" as my son learned to do during this test. Months later, when I picked him up from school, he began to tell me about his day. He casually ended with, "Mommy, I was told that my name is on the list to be recognized by the Ministry of Education, which means I probably got a top score in one of the subjects." As it turned out, he had not only received the top score in one subject but rather in two, namely Mathematics and Health Science. At the awards ceremony he was among the few who received plaques for two subject awards. These honors were even greater than the recognition he had missed, because it meant that out of all of the thousands of students who had taken the exam, he would have gotten the highest score in the country while taking them a year earlier. He was so elated and so were we. I reminded him of what God had said earlier: "all things work together for the good..." I said, you see, God always gets the last say! We are still praising God for the victory He brought to our son.

When we leave challenges in God's hands, trust Him and continue to be faithful in His work, God's peace transcends and in His time He makes all things beautiful. Remember, when Abraham was asked by God to sacrifice Isaac, his son of promise? He prepared Isaac for sacrifice and was prepared to do what God asked without wavering, knowing that God was faithful to raise Isaac from the dead if He had to. Abraham had God's peace as he walked up Mount Moriah. Just before he was about to slay his son, God's angel called out to him telling him not to do it, that he had proven that he would be faithful to do whatever God asked. Then God provided a ram caught in a thicket for the sacrifice and spared Isaac's life. Abraham fully trusted God and walked in peace and obedience and God provided what he needed and right on time. When we walk in God's supernatural peace, His provision and power will be manifested in our lives!

As we conclude this chapter, I would again like to share a story from my favorite T.V. show *Monk*. In the episode, "Mr. Monk and the Astronaut", Adrian Monk, the world famous detective, was taunted by an astronaut who was suspected of murder. This astronaut was brave and appeared to be fearless. He had even carried out an emergency space shuttle landing in the middle of the ocean. He was trying to intimidate Monk because Monk discovered he was in fact the killer. In one of the scenes, while bragging about how brave he was and how fearful Monk was, he intentionally flicked his fingers unexpectedly in Monk's face to get him to flinch in fear and Monk did. Then, he told Monk that he was a flincher and when things got tough, he would always flinch. At the end of the episode, when Monk cracked the case, the astronaut tried to escape by aircraft to dispose of a critical piece of evidence. Monk sprinted down the runway and stood in the plane's pathway. The astronaut continued to move forward, bringing the plane's nose to within inches of Monk's face expecting Monk to flinch. This time Monk stood firm and refused to be moved or shaken and faced his fear.

In life, the enemy will taunt us in an effort to get us to flinch in fear and abandon our God-ordained purpose. Remember, we have The Most High God on our side. We don't have to be bound by the spirit of fear that causes us to flinch, worry or become anxious, but we can stand boldly in the face of any adversity, knowing that we have God our Perfect Protector, Peace, Provider and Pioneer on our side giving us Perfect Positioning in this race of life!

> But now, God's Message, the God who made you in the first place, Jacob, the One who got you started, Israel: "Don't be afraid, I've redeemed you. I've called your name. You're mine. When you're in over your head, I'll be there with you. When you're in rough waters, you will not go down. When you're between a rock and a hard place, it won't be a dead end— Because I am God, your personal God, The Holy of Israel, your Savior. I paid a huge price for you: all of Egypt, with rich Cush and Seba thrown in! That's how much you mean to me! That's how much I love you! I'd sell off the whole world to get you back, trade the creation just for you. (Isaiah 43:1-3 MSG)

The promise God made to Israel is the same promise He makes to us when we receive Jesus as our Savior and make Him our Lord. We are engrafted into His family and become children of the Most High God with full access to all His blessings. We, therefore, have no cause for worry or alarm, for God is with us and for us!

CHAPTER 11

DON'T ABORT THE VISION

As we run our course, we must keep this one truth at the forefront of our minds: God has created each of us with a purpose in mind, and we were born with the potential to accomplish this purpose and finish our race. He desires to birth something special and priceless in and through us, so that we can make our contribution on planet earth.

Get ready for divine deposits

As we run our course, we must prepare ourselves for the increase and deposits that God has in store for us along the way.

> Clear lots of ground for your tents! Make your tents large. Spread out! Think big! Use plenty of rope, drive the tent pegs deep. You're going to need lots of elbow room for your growing family. You're going to take over whole nations; you're going to resettle abandoned cities.
>
> (Isaiah 54:2-3 MSG)

I believe our "growing family" refers to the ministry that God wants to birth through us which will be our area of influence. He says we are going to take over whole nations, which I believe means we are going to demolish the strongholds of the enemy in those areas and set the captives free with God's Word and power. We are also going to resettle abandoned cities, which involves infusing places that have been discarded and forgotten with the presence of God we carry within us.

There are divine deposits God wants to make in the earth through each one of us as we go along, so that others may see His glory because we have passed their way. These deposits may come in the form of songs, books, messages, rehabilitation programs, witty inventions, medical discoveries or simply words of encouragement and extending a helping hand to someone in need. There is so much God wants to do through us that we have to make space for the vision that He has destined for us to fulfill. Therefore, we have to prepare ourselves to receive the miracles God wants to birth through us. The above scripture also tells us to think big. Why? God is a big God and He wants to accomplish great things on the earth so that people will see His mighty acts and believe in His supernatural power to save, heal and set them free from their yokes and burdens!

However, there are several steps that we must embrace before we can receive the vision God has destined for us to birth. We must remember that God is a God of process and nothing happens overnight. Just like the farmer plants the seed into the ground and it goes through a process of germination and will only blossom in the right environment, the seed that God plants in our hearts must go through a similar process.

The divine commitment

Before we can ever receive God's vision for our lives, we must be in right relationship with Him through a relationship with Jesus Christ, His Son. Jesus is the bridge between God and ourselves and when we accept His perfect sacrifice on Calvary's cross, then we have full access to God and all the blessings He has in store for us.

Many who run the race of life do not want to fully commit themselves to God. They just want to date God and keep their options open, thinking that something better may come along. They are only interested in experiencing cheap thrills here and there.

A lot of runners stay in this zone, courting God occasionally, when it is convenient for them, or especially when they are in a tight spot or there is a need in their life. However, what they do not realize is that God wants more than that. He requires unwavering commitment from us. He wants us to be in a spiritual marriage relationship with Him. He has so much to deposit in us, but it can only occur in this type of relationship.

The Apostle Paul refers to us (the church) being the bride of Christ in Ephesians 5.

> For no one ever hated his own flesh, but nourishes and cherishes it, just as the Lord does the church. For we are members of His body, of His flesh and of His bones. "For this reason a man shall leave his father and mother and be joined to his wife, and the two shall become one flesh." This is a great mystery, but I speak concerning Christ and the church.
>
> (Ephesians 5:29-32 NKJV)

The divine conception

Just as there should be ongoing intimacy in a human marriage, God desires intimacy in our marriage relationship with Him. This is the only way He can deposit His seed in our lives. There is no conception without intimacy. In our intimate times of worship with the Lord, He plants the seed of greatness in our spiritual wombs. The Bible says, "In His presence there is fullness of joy and at His right hand there are pleasures forever more." When the potential God has created in us fuses with the seed He deposits in us during our times of intimacy with Him, conception of His vision and purpose for our lives takes place.

This happened to Paul in Acts 9 after his Damascus experience with the Lord. In verse 11, God told Ananias "to go to the House of Judas on Straight Street and ask for a man from Tarsus name Saul, for he is praying." Do you know what was taking place during that time of praying – intimacy that led to conception. He received his instructions to evangelize the Gentile regions of the world. His assignment was birthed in those moments of intimacy.

Saul was ripe and ready to receive the seed that God wanted to deposit in him. All that was needed was his divine commitment that took place on the way to Damascus (Acts 9:1-8) and intimate time spent with God in Judas' home. At this time, the vision was conceived in his heart.

Have we been intimate with God and conceived in our heart the vision that God wants to accomplish through us? If the answer in "No" then we have been running this race in vain. We are running without a purpose and we don't know where our destination is. So we run aimlessly and frustrated. There is no better time than the present to spend time in God's presence and become intimately acquainted with His will for lives.

The divine carrying

If we have experienced this intimacy and subsequent conception, then we like Paul have become pregnant with the vision of God.

God told Ananias in verse 15, "Go! This man is my chosen instrument to proclaim My name to the Gentiles and their kings and to the people of Israel. I will show him how much he must suffer for My name."

Just like an expectant mother realizes she is carrying a very important package the moment she becomes aware that she's pregnant, it is the same with us when we realize we are pregnant with destiny. We recognize that we are carrying God's precious bundle of joy He has prepared for this world. This means we have to take care of ourselves because whatever we do, affects the life "within us".

Sometimes we want to carry this baby for God, but we are bombarded with challenges such as sickness, weariness, over-exhaustion, poverty, lack, fear, worry and doubt and we are threatened with a spiritual miscarriage. Look at how many setbacks Paul experienced. As we learned earlier, he was stoned, shipwrecked, beaten, imprisoned, thrown out of cities and a myriad of others things. However, this was his response to the hardships he faced:

> We are hard pressed on every side, but not crushed; perplexed, but not in despair; persecuted, but not abandoned; stuck down; but not destroyed… Therefore we do not lose heart. Though outwardly we are wasting away, yet inwardly we are being renewed day by day. For our light and momentary troubles are achieving for us an eternal glory that far outweighs them all. So we fix our eyes not on what is seen, but what is unseen, since what is seen is temporary, but what is unseen is eternal.
>
> (2 Corinthians 4:8-9; 14-16 NIV)

We are carrying God's vision that He has determined to birth through us. This vision has a right to live and a right to be born. Therefore, God is encouraging us to not abort the vision that He has planted in us. Some of us know what our calling is, we can see it right now, but because of the spiritual morning sickness we experience as a result of carrying the vision, we want to abort our purpose. There have been many days in my life where the challenges have been great, whether it be financial, relational, physical, mental or emotional, but I knew the pressures I was facing were a direct result of my determination to pursue God's will for my life. Sometimes, I questioned if it was really worth it, because I was tired and weary and did not feel like encountering one more difficulty. It was in these times that I took my burdens to the Lord and poured out all of my disappointments, doubts and despair to Him. As I laid my concerns at His feet, I began to worship Him and wait for His instructions on my next steps. He always gave me words of hope and I arose empowered to continue the race.

God is there to strengthen us in our times of weakness. In 2 Corinthians 12:9, Paul experienced God's supernatural power in his time of weakness. Paul had a thorn in the flesh that He pleaded with the Lord to take away. God's answer to him was "My grace is sufficient for you, for my power is made perfect in weakness." Paul had an awesome responsibility and if it was going to be accomplished, it was going to be accomplished God's way through His strength and power not Paul's. Even though Paul faced many obstacles in pursuit of his purpose, every time he experienced weakness, God provided the strength that he needed when he needed it. Therefore, when Paul accomplished his mission, he boasted in the Lord, because he knew it was God Who brought him through.

Do you feel weak right now, like you can't make it another minute, let alone another day? Then rely on God's power to see you through in this moment. Step out in faith and continue to run your race and the power of God will come upon you and rise up within you as you go. God promises us in Hebrews 13:5, "Never will I leave you; never will I forsake you." In the next verse, we find our appropriate response, "So we say with confidence, the Lord is my helper; I will not be afraid. What can mere mortals do to me?" We have to endure the trials because it is only for a season. Have you ever seen anyone experience morning sickness after the baby has been born?

Now during pregnancy there is expansion according to the passage in Isaiah we read at the beginning of this chapter. There is much preparation and excitement, especially if it is the first pregnancy. I remember when I wrote my first book, I was so excited, I couldn't wait to see the finished copy. When I held it in my hands, I was so thankful and expectant of what God would do through the words He had given me. I thought about the lives that had been impacted by rape and abuse that would receive healing and deliverance. I rejoiced in the Lord and the great things He had done in and through me!

However, to get to this point of birthing, there is much discomfort: sometimes we cannot move as quickly, we frequently take bathroom breaks, sometimes our feet swell, sometimes we feel dizzy and there are many sleepless nights. Our body is sacrificed of almost all comfort for the safety and protection of the baby. Just as it is not easy carrying a human baby, it is definitely not easy carrying a God conceived vision to full term. However, with God's help we can deliver successfully.

The divine birthing

Past all of the morning sickness, thoughts of abortion, and threatened miscarriages, we arrive at the ninth month, the time where our cords have been enlarged to the maximum. We roll when we walk. We need help getting out of bed. We can't stand up for long periods of time. Nothing fits us. We are most uncomfortable at this time and the fetus has fully matured and is ready to come out in Jesus' name and breathe on its own. No more incubation is needed. And so the cervix thins, there may be spotting, and the first signs of labour begin. The baby makes its descent through the spiritual birth canal. The water bag is burst by the Great Physician, the uterus is contracting and you are moaning and groaning because you are experiencing extreme pain and discomfort. It has been said that the pain that is experienced during childbirth can be so severe that a woman has one foot in the grave and the other out. But "we shall not die but live to declare the Glory of the Lord" (Psalm 118:17).

Then there comes the point where we have dilated the full ten centimeters and it's now time to push GOD'S BABY OUT. And you get in the birth position and push like you have never pushed before until there is crowning, that is when the head of the baby appears. Then the pushing must be intensified with all you've got with the encouragement of your spiritual spouse, GOD HIMSELF and all involved in the birth process. Then, the baby plops out. It is here, breathing on its own, kicking and screaming, and letting the world know I AM HERE and I'VE GOT A JOB TO DO.

Push past the discomfort

This is why we are running, and therefore we must be patient and remain focused. The vision God wants to birth in us has an appointed time. During the course of our lives, we will experience difficulties and we wonder whether we were ever called, if we really heard from God and if what He said would happen would really come to pass. This is the time when we must hang in there and trust God even when we can't trace Him. Because we know His character as a result of spending time in His presence, we can be confident that even though the way seems dark, God will show up in the nick of time and do what He said He would do. That is why we can't give up on the vision or purpose God has for us to fulfill. No matter how hard the opposition in our lives has been, and no matter how many times we have been knocked down by the winds of adversity – the time is now for us to get back up and continue to run our race!

I am reminded of the motion picture *Rocky*[4], starring Sylvester Stallone, who played a boxing champion. At the end of the movie, Rocky finds himself in the fight of his life with a Russian opponent. Rocky is pinned to the ground with the referee about to make the third and final count to declare his opponent the champion. It is at this point when Rocky remembers who he is and the power he possesses, and he makes a mental determination to press through the present pain and humiliation of the moment and find the inner strength to get back up and fight. He arises as he begins to fight back, defeats his opponent and is declared the boxing champion.

It is the same with us. In this race, we sometimes feel like we are in a boxing match. The challenges we face feel like blows and are all out attempts to throw us off course from arriving at our destination. We may be black and blue from the punches of life and the referee may be giving us the final count, 3, 2... However, something deep down inside of us rises up and we refuse to give up, surrender or die.

We must ask ourselves, what will cause us to keep going after we have faced so many challenges or obstacles to fulfilling our purpose. The answer to this question, I believe, is found in the Old Testament.

> And then God answered: write this. Write what you see. Write it out in big block letters so that it can be read on the run. This vision-message is a witness pointing to what's coming. It aches for the coming - it can

hardly wait! And it doesn't lie. If it seems slow in coming, wait. It's on the way. It will come in right on time. (Habakkuk 2:2-3 MSG)

God has big plans for His children and no matter what opposition we face, He says to hold on to the Word He has given us, because even if it appears to tarry, He promises it will surely come to pass in His timing and His way. That is why we should write it down in big letters so that every time we get faint in the race, we can refer to what God has promised and read it quickly while we run.

We must refuse to abort the vision God has birthed in us, and get back up and fight for God's purpose in us to live, move and change the world that we live in! God's Holy Spirit ignites the heart and fire of the vision He has planted in us and we have to arise because we know, "it can't end like this", with us being defeated and not finishing our course. It is with every fiber of our spiritual being that we will begin to get up in faith believing that "greater is He (God) that is in us, than he that is within the world" (1 John 4:4). We can face our enemies and challenges and overcome our obstacles because of how big, strong and mighty our God is!

So keep the faith and stay in the race!

CHAPTER 12

THE POWER WITHIN

*N*ow that we have made the decision to hold on to the vision and stay in the race, it is essential that we realize Who is empowering us to do what we do – GOD HIMSELF! Many times, we can get so comfortable doing what we do, that we sometimes forget that it is indeed God's power that enables us to leave a footprint on this earth. Other times, we get so caught up in our own lives and situations that we fail to see the bigger picture, and we miss God's promptings to fulfill a role that is a part of us running a successful race in His eyes, not the world's or our own. What God qualifies as success is the only thing that really matters, and it is only then when we see His mighty power at work in our lives, that we recognize that it is "not by might, nor by power but by His Spirit" (Zechariah 4:6) that we get to do the things we do.

So God has birthed a vision or purpose in us, but how is it going to be accomplished? First, we must recognize that God's purpose is bigger than our lives and what we consider important. It is bigger than our jobs, professions, education, businesses – things that keep us busy every day and keep our minds so preoccupied.

Opposition from without or within

Some of us in our journey will sense the call of God to do something out of the ordinary. We know God is calling us to something higher and bigger than ourselves. It was like that for me when I penned my first book. God led me to leave my job and write this book that would be a source of healing and restoration to many others who would have experienced the trauma and pain of rape and sexual abuse. All the pieces of the puzzle were not in place and at that time my husband's job was made redundant and he had only just found another job, so financial stability was an issue. However, I stepped out in faith in obedience to the call God had on my life, and my book was birthed and published within two years.

Other times in our lives, God may want us to do something for Him, but either we don't see it or feel under qualified or incapable of doing what He is asking. Therefore, we make excuses so that we can get out of it. Many times our unwillingness to step out is based on the fact that we feel we need to have all of the answers or resources before we take that first step.

In each of these cases, we must recognize that God is the One Who has called us and He is the One Who will provide the resources and strength to enable us to fulfill our role, thereby running a successful course. The stories of two Biblical characters come to mind as I attempt to unpack this point.

Be concerned about what God is concerned about

In the story of Nehemiah in the Old Testament, God had placed a burden on Nehemiah's heart concerning the broken down state of the walls of Jerusalem. Nehemiah was a Jew, who was living in exile in the foreign citadel of Susa holding a very influential post as the cupbearer to the king. He had it made and things were going well for him, but God had something bigger for him to do. When he was informed about the ruins in Jerusalem, he wept before the Lord for his homeland and his brothers and sisters who were suffering. It was during this time that the purpose of rebuilding the walls and city gates of Jerusalem and securing the city itself was birthed in his heart. He was living in comfort while the city of his God lay in shambles.

Nehemiah knew that God was calling him for a higher assignment. However, how was he going to accomplish this? He was in a foreign land working under a foreign king? He couldn't just leave and attend to this new call. He spent time fasting and praying for the favor to be able to do what God was requiring of him.

The king appreciated Nehemiah's work and soon recognized that he was bothered about something. When Nehemiah explained the reason for his sad countenance, he won the favor of the king and queen and was allowed to go to take care of his Heavenly Father's business. Nehemiah prayed for God's favor to be allowed to take care of God's work and that is exactly what happened. Not only did the king allow him to go and fulfill his purpose, but he also provided him with letters to take to all of the governors through whose towns he would travel, and armed guards to ensure his safety. He was also given a letter to procure all of the wood needed to rebuild the walls.

What God calls for, He truly provides for. Nehemiah was willing to step out in faith because he knew Who was backing him. Likewise, we just have to be willing to step out and embrace the call and remember that it is God that does the providing and empowering. When we keep Him at the forefront of all our plans, we will succeed in accomplishing His purpose for our lives, thereby running a successful race!

Leadership is the key

Nehemiah was an excellent leader. He returned to Jerusalem and quietly surveyed the damage and determined how the work could be done effectively. However, he didn't share this vision with anyone there until his assessment was completed and his plan devised.

Sometimes, we open our mouths too quickly and prematurely share the things we have heard God say He wants us to do. This is the time for planning and preparation and we must give the vision a time to incubate. If we open our mouths, there may be someone around us who may try to discourage us or suggest that we are incapable of completing the task we have been asked to do. We can't share our plans with everyone, sometimes even with those who will be a part of the work before the appointed time.

Be prepared for opposition

Nehemiah learned, and so will we, that opposition to God's plan usually comes immediately. However, it is just a test to see if we will have the tenacity to forge ahead no matter what. If we continue to press, then God knows we are serious about our goal and determined to get to the finish line. In the case of Nehemiah, he faced resistance from two men, Sanballot and Tobias, who were foreigners to Israel and resistant to its success. They became aware of Nehemiah's determination to work on behalf of the people of Israel. They took exception to his work. However, the vision had been firmly planted in Nehemiah's heart and his faith in God prevailed when he responded to their insults.

> When Sanballat, Tobiah, and an Arab named Geshem heard what we were planning to do, they laughed at us and said, "What do you think you're doing? Are you going to rebel against the emperor?" I answered, "The God of Heaven will give us success. We are his servants, and we are going to start building. But you have no right to any property in Jerusalem, and you have no share in its traditions."
>
> (Nehemiah 2:19-20 GNT)

This statement to his enemies clearly demonstrated that his hope was in God and God alone to finish the work he had been given to do. Then Nehemiah reminded his opponents that what he was doing had nothing to do with them and it was none of their business. He was bold and radical about the race he had chosen to run.

148

Stand firm in the face of opposition

We, as believers in Jesus Christ, must also possess Nehemiah's radical kind of faith in God's power in our lives that gives us the ability to get the job done. Then we must also possess the boldness and tenacity to let our enemies know that what we are doing for God is not dependent on whether they agree with us or not. It's really no concern of theirs; therefore they need only to stand and watch what God is going to do through us. We too often let other people's opinions govern our God-given purpose.

Look at Noah. He built the ark without ever seeing a drop of rain. If he had listened to the naysayers of his time, he and his family would have been destroyed in the flood.

The question is this: Can God depend on you to complete His work no matter what the setbacks or the voices of opposition, criticism or indifference may be?

Know that God is your power within

What happens when the verbal insults turn into physical threats? Nehemiah also experienced this. Tobias and Sanballot were devising plans to harm Nehemiah and his workers in an effort to prevent him from finishing the work. Our opponents may sometimes try to do whatever it takes to derail us and frighten us from the task we have been given. However, God will give us the wisdom we need to overcome the obstacles we face to continue to run our race. In the case of Nehemiah, God led him to have half of the builders become warriors and even those who continued in the building process were armed. He also had armed guards in the city at night. When his followers became afraid, God gave Nehemiah words of comfort and assurance for them.

> Don't be afraid of our enemies. Remember how great and terrifying the Lord is, and fight for your relatives, your children, your wives and your homes. (Nehemiah 4:14 GNT)

Again Nehemiah displayed excellent leadership and reminded them, and indeed himself, that the God they served was mighty and was fighting for them. God had called them to this work and He would provide whatever protection they needed along the way. God had them covered. He was the Power Within that would give them overcoming ability to press through into victory. And… their enemies' plans were squashed.

This is indeed a lesson for us. When God places an assignment in our hearts, He will give us the wisdom and power to defeat our enemies, overcome the hurdles in our way and finish with class and distinction like Nehemiah did. However, we must recognize that it is God, not us, Who does the calling and empowering in this race of our lives. True success is only found in Him!

In the case of Nehemiah, He knew what God wanted him to do, and he prepared himself mentally and threw himself wholeheartedly into the work he had been given. His opposition came from without – other people tried to prevent him from forging ahead.

See what God sees

What happens when God has a job that He has assigned us to do, but we don't believe we have what it takes to accomplish what He is asking of us? The opposition we face is then internal. It lies in our failure to believe that God is empowering us. This was the case with Gideon, whose story is relayed in Judges chapters 6-8.

In this story, we learn that Israel was in captivity to the Midianites because they had sinned against the Lord. They were being exploited and they cried out to the Lord. God heard their cry and moved to deliver them out of bondage as He had done through Moses when they were in Egypt.

This time God chose to work through a man called Gideon. When God visited Gideon in the winepress, He called to him saying, "The

Lord is with you, brave and mighty man" (Judges 6:12 GNT). God referred to Gideon the way He saw him, who He had created him to be – a mighty warrior.

Gideon, however, saw himself quite differently. When God informed him of his mission – which was to use his great strength to rescue Israel from the Midianites – it was as if Gideon looked around and wondered who God was talking to. Gideon did not see himself as the warrior God saw and gave the Lord strong evidence as to why He was speaking to the "wrong man". Gideon replies:

> But, Lord, how can I rescue Israel? My clan is the weakest in the tribe of Manasseh, and I am the least important member of my family.
> (Judges 6:15 GNT)

In essence, Gideon was telling God, "You have the wrong man. Not only is my tribe the weakest, but I am also the weakest in my clan. Look for someone else. I am incapable of doing what you have asked. I don't have it in me."

Isn't that similar to us sometimes in this race we run? God has some pretty amazing things for us to do, and we look at what disqualifies us from fulfilling our role. Like Gideon, we come up with all kinds of excuses as to why we are not the one to use.

God knows what He has placed within us. He lives in us so we are more than capable of accomplishing His purpose for our lives. God is telling us, "It's in you, because I am in you." It is God Who is empowering us to get the job done and we must stand on His command to do what He has predestined us to do. Many times, God will refrain from using the ones who appear to be strong in their own might or think they have it all together.

> But God chose the foolish things of the world to shame the wise; God chose the weak things of this world to shame the strong. God chose the lowly things of this world and the despised things – and the things that are not – to nullify the things that are, so that no one would boast before Him. Therefore it is written: Let the one who boasts, boast in the Lord. (1 Corinthians 1:27-28, 31 NIV)

God knows that by ourselves we don't qualify, but connected to Him we are more than conquerors to do mighty things by His grace – His supernatural power that enables us to press!

We can do all things through Christ!

This is what He had to show Gideon and many times this is what He is trying to get us to see and embrace. By ourselves we are nothing, but with God all things are possible. Remember, David was the least likely of Jesse's sons to be the next king of Israel or to face the giant Goliath, but he was the one God chose and used greatly on Israel's behalf.

"Man sees the outside but God looks at the heart" (1 Samuel 16:7). God tells us to "be strong in the Lord and in the power of His might" (Ephesians 6:10) and "I can do all things through Christ who gives me strength" (Philippians 4:13). If we are going to successfully do what we have been created to do, we must rely on God's strength and ability. It's as simple as that. We may need to refocus our lens to see what God sees in us so that we can have the faith to step out and be who He has called us to be.

A fleece test

In Gideon's case, he needed a few signs to assure him that God was calling him to this great work. It wasn't that Gideon did not want to rescue Israel, but rather he wanted to make certain that it was indeed God Who was leading him to do so. Therefore, he conducted a fleece test. He put a piece of fleece on the floor and asked God to let the dew of the night fill the fleece only but not the ground around it by the next morning. The next morning, what Gideon asked for was exactly what happened. Then in the final test, Gideon asked the Lord to let the ground around the fleece be filled with dew the next morning, but not the fleece. Again, God did exactly that. God wasn't angry or impatient about these tests either. He knew that it wasn't that Gideon was unwilling, but he was afraid to step out unless he had God's full assurance that He was with him.

Sometimes we may be uncertain that we are hearing from God. We can follow Gideon's example and ask God for specific signs to confirm His purpose for our lives. God understands our weaknesses and apprehensions and He will be glad to confirm what He has called us to do. At least, we are not rejecting the request without even considering it. However, when He confirms it we must be willing to act with boldness and without delay, like Gideon did.

Victory will be achieved God's way

Once Gideon knew he had God's backing, he immediately got his men together and was ready to seize the Midianite army. Then God intervened again and told Gideon that he had too many men to fight against their enemies. When this battle would have been fought and won, it would be completely evident that it was the Lord Who empowered them and gave them the victory. God reduced the size of Gideon's army from 30,000 to 300 men. In the natural this would have spelled obvious disaster, but because God was their strength and power, the Israelites prevailed over the Midianites who fled in fear and eventually destroyed each other. God knew what He had placed in Gideon. Therefore, He worked with Gideon until Gideon saw and embraced the Power that was within him.

What has God been asking of you? Maybe it's time to conduct a fleece test of some sort so that you can get your confirmation. Remember the plans that God has for us are "good and not to harm you, plans to give you a hope and a future" (Jeremiah 29:11). They are usually bigger than what we can accomplish on our own, and so we must constantly recognize, acknowledge and embrace the power within us – our Great, All-Powerful God.

Both Nehemiah and Gideon had a race to run and faced obstacles along the way, whether external forces or internal struggles. However, the key to their success lied in them realizing that God lived in them and would empower them to do what He had called them to do. He was their answer and source of overcoming power in the race "that was set before them". He was the "author and finisher of their faith" (Hebrews 12:2).

It is the same with us. God's Spirit lives in us and will empower us to complete our assignment and run a successful race for Him. He has the answer to all of the obstacles and hindrances we will face on our course. All we have to do is recognize Who is backing us and know we have the power to "walk unharmed among lions and snakes, and kick young lions and serpents from the path" (Psalm 91:13) as we run on to a flourishing finish.

You are a king

One final note: no matter where you are, even if you feel you have failed God or yourself, don't give up. Get back up and continue to run your race. In the movie, *The Lion King*[5], Simba the young lion cub felt he was responsible for the death of his father, Mufasseh, the Lion King. He was tricked into believing this by his jealous uncle Scar, who was, in fact, the actual killer. As a result, Simba ran from his purpose of becoming the next Lion King of his pride and wandered around the jungle with a warthog and a meerkat, animals he was not supposed to play with but rather rule. He was out of place and the pride he was supposed to manage was on the brink of disaster. His dead father had to visit him in a vision to let him know that "he was more than he had become. He needed to remember that he was a king." When Simba received this reminder, he responded with great tenacity, defeated his uncle, saved his pride and took his rightful place as the true Lion King.

Your Heavenly Father wants you to remember who you are right now.

You are a king. He desires for you to especially remember Whose you are. If you have accepted Jesus Christ, then you belong to God's family and you are assured of His protection and provision. Arise today and defend your pride – that is, your area of influence – and finish strong!

If you haven't accepted Jesus Christ as your Lord and Savior, you can do that right now. Just bow your head and say this prayer:

> *Lord Jesus, I repent of my sins. I ask that You forgive me and come into my heart and be my Savior and Lord. I confess with my mouth that Jesus is Lord and I believe this truth in my heart. Thank You for saving me today and welcoming me into Your family. In Jesus' Name I pray, Amen!*

If you just said that prayer, you are now a part of the family of God. You are indeed a king. Tell somebody about your commitment today and join a Bible believing church so that you can grow and mature in your faith in Christ and experience the Power Within!

CONCLUSION

A FIGHT TO THE FINISH: IT'S IN THE PRESS

*M*y family is a track family. We love watching track and field and have been taping the Olympics and World Games since 1999. Both of our kids have been involved in track and field for many years, so we have had the opportunity of watching many races and understand what it takes to run a successful race.

The goal of every runner in the race is to win. In order to win, one must cross the finish line first. This person will be declared the champion of that race.

In the Christian race, we are also running for a prize and in order to receive it we must finish the race. The difference between the natural race and the spiritual race is that with the spiritual race when we finish our race we automatically win first place. This is because we are the only ones who can complete the race we have been chosen by God to run.

Over the years, I have seen many athletes finish fast and strong. However, there were others who had challenges along the way, but did not give up and pressed through to finish. The important thing to note is that they finished the race.

In this race of our lives, there will be difficulties, challenges and obstacles, but with God on our side empowering us, WE WILL FINISH THE RACE AND WIN THE PRIZE!

The apostle Paul encouraged himself to press through the difficulties:

> I'm not saying that I have this all together, that I have it made. But I am well on my way, reaching out for Christ, who has so wondrously reached out for me. Friends, don't get me wrong: By no means do I count myself an expert in all this, but I've got my eyes on the goal, where God is beckoning us onward – to Jesus. I'm off and running and I'm not turning back. (Philippians 3:12-14 MSG)

The NIV says, "But I press on to take hold of that for which Christ Jesus took hold of me."

So we have to make up our minds that no matter what, WE WILL PRESS and not stop until we finish this race. Sometimes, it will take all you have within you to press through. Pressing is an uncomfortable process. In a race, it is a decision to strain and forge ahead despite the resistance and physical agony you experience.

The lesson from the grape

The analogy of making grape juice or wine is also applicable here. In order to get the juice out of the grape, the grape must go through the process of pressing. This involves either stamping or squeezing the grape until all of its essence is extracted. The juice is then processed and preserved for immediate or future use. If it is to be used for wine, this liquid can be preserved for decades, long after the grape is gone. The grape then becomes a raisin and is useful for "clearing out clogged passages." So even the swiveled grape still has a purpose.

When we press or are pressed, we must recognize that we are being squeezed and strained, so that all of our essence, that is all of our gifts and purpose, can be extracted from us to be used by God so His glory is manifested on the earth! If we remain in grape form, our usefulness will be short lived because grapes decay quickly. However, if we allow ourselves to be pressed, the juice or essence of our lives will last long after we are gone. Even when we become a swiveled raisin, we are still useful in helping others clear their blocked passages so that they can press, be pressed, finish their course and receive their prize as well.

The Finish Line

Paul sensed when his race was about to be finished. He knew when he had completed his work. At the end of his life he was able to say, "The time of my departure is at hand. I have fought a good fight, I have run my course and I have kept the faith." And he knew what was waiting for him. He didn't say it in agony or fear, but he embraced the end because he knew that he had completed his work and he looked forward to his reward. He finished, that's why he could face the end with great joy. Trials and hardships didn't cause Paul to lose his focus or abort his mission.

> And now, compelled by the Spirit, I am going to Jerusalem, not knowing what will happen to me there. I only know that in every city the Holy Spirit warns me that prison and hardships are facing me. However, I consider my life worth nothing to me, if only I may finish the race and complete the task of testifying to the gospel of God's grace.
>
> (Acts 20:22-24 NIV)

Keep your eyes on the prize

Will we have this type of testimony at the end of our journey? Can we press through and overcome the obstacles that we face, fight to the finish all the while believing that "God is able to do exceeding abundantly above all that we can ever ask or think or even imagine (Ephesian 3:20)" and that "it is he who endures to the end that will be saved (Matthew 24:13). Paul realized this. That is why he said, "He beats his body and brings it under subjection, so that after leading others to the contest, he himself would not be disqualified" (1 Corinthians 9:27).

The whole Gentile world was depending on Paul to overcome and finish. Today, many are counting on us to overcome and finish.

Let us "run with patience the run that is set before us, keeping our eyes on Jesus, the author and finisher of our faith" (Hebrews 12:2).

When we finish our race and leave this earth fully spent out, our loving Heavenly Father will both recognize and receive us into His arms declaring, "Well done, thy good and faithful servant" (Matthew 25:23). The angelic host and all those who have gone before us will also celebrate our arrival.

What a glorious day that will be!

SMALL GROUP STUDY GUIDE

The Ultimate Six-Session Study Guide to Understanding and Overcoming Struggles in Life

All of us seek to discover how to successfully run the race we have been assigned and master the hand we have been dealt. Believers sometimes begin to doubt their faith because their life is filled with so many hurdles. The truth is life isn't easy for anybody. Challenges often appear overwhelming and insurmountable. Even if you are secure in your own faith, it can be difficult to help others who are struggling.

This excellent small group experience is a six session road map to victory. Also a great resource for individual study, this guide will give you key strategies to overcome and to keep fighting until you reach your finish line.

Each session includes…

- ⛶ Key Verse
- ☻ Food for Thought
- ▶ Video Lesson
- ⌾ Discussion Questions
- ⚓ Anchor Verse
- ◉ Going Deeper
- 🙏 Weekly Devotional

Start a group, today, using this easy to facilitate format. Allow God to empower you through the pages of this guide as well as the meaningful discussions that will occur in your small group sessions. The sooner you get this guide the sooner you will have the tools you need to successfully lead a group and give them the strength to leave their past hurts behind and embrace the gratifying future that comes from persevering.

Overcoming Obstacles Small Group Study Guide[6]
ISBN 978-1-56229-246-1
Volume discounts available

ENDNOTES

[1] Muccino, G. (Director). (2006). *The Pursuit of Happyness* [Motion picture on DVD]. Columbia Tristar Home Entertainment.

[2] Breckman, A. (Producer). (2002, July 12). *Monk* [Television series]. USA Network.

[3] Edgecombe, T. (2005). *A Time to Heal: Restoration from the Ravages of Rape*. Largo, Maryland: Christian Living Books, Inc. Available in paperback and eBook formats from ChristianLivingBooks.com or wherever books are sold.

[4] Avildsen, J. (Director). (1981). *Rocky* [Motion picture on DVD]. RCA SelectaVision VideoDiscs.

[5] Allers, R. (Director). (1994). *The Lion King* [Motion picture on DVD]. The Walt Disney Co.

[6] Edgecombe, T. and Edgecombe, A. (2016). *Overcoming Obstacles Small Group Study Guide*. Largo, Maryland: Christian Living Books, Inc. Available from ChristianLivingBooks.com, the authors or wherever books are sold.

Made in the USA
Middletown, DE
10 October 2023

40571451R00097